What's In Your Toolbox?

Building A Strong Spiritual Foundation In Jesus Christ

Deacon Glenn And Linda Harmon

Blessings,

Deacon Glenn & Linda

Published by BookLocker.com, Inc. Bradenton, Florida, U.S.A.

Printed on acid-free paper.

BookLocker.com, Inc.
2016

First Edition

Glenn Harmon Ministries
625 Zaharias Circle
Hemet, CA. 92545
337-515-9224

www.glennharmonministries.org
apostlesforjesus@yahoo.org

Disclaimer

This book is based on the authors' personal experiences with their Christian faith, offering those experiences as inspirations to readers who are searching for faith, or renewed faith, in their Catholic Christian tradition.

Glenn Harmon is an ordained Deacon in the Roman Catholic Church and his wife, Linda, is a devote Catholic who accompanies her husband on their missions and retreats across the United States and Canada.

Their stories focus on how God's revelations of His goodness and mercy in their lives inspired them to dedicate their lives to spreading the Gospel of Jesus Christ through more than 500 parish missions over more than 20 years, providing faith-filled insights about living a Christian life filled with God's joy, peace, inspiration and comfort.

Neither the authors or publisher, nor any contributors or other representatives will be liable for damages arising out of or in connection with the use of this book. This is a comprehensive limitation of liability that applies to all damages of any kind, including (without limitation) compensatory; direct, indirect or consequential damages; loss of data, income or profit; loss of damage to property and claims of third parties.

This book provides content related to religious topics and the personal experiences of its authors. As such, use of this book implies your acceptance of this disclaimer.

Dedication

We dedicate this book, first and foremost, to Our Lord Jesus Christ. His guidance and support, as well as His mercy, love, healing and forgiveness changed our lives. We hope and pray that the words on these pages will give Him glory and honor and bless people everywhere.

We also dedicate this book to all our family and friends who have stood by us with their prayers and support.

Linda and I are deeply grateful for John and Roberta Wolcott, who poured their hearts and souls into this effort. Their professional guidance in all aspects of writing and publication has been invaluable. Without their hard work this book would not have been possible.

Our thanks also go out to our dear friends John and Sharon Somers and Linda Mars. Their suggestions and editing efforts added an invaluable element to this book.

Also, Linda and I appreciate Bob Higgins for his amazing artist drawing of our Lord Jesus Christ and his permission to use it in this book.

Table of Contents

Introduction

Jesus Christ made two promises about building a strong spiritual foundation.

So why is it so important, and necessary, to explore these two promises made more than 2,000 years ago in a distant country?

By now you have probably learned that none of us can avoid the difficulties of life. In other words, we cannot escape the cross!

Each day we're faced with challenges which can create stress, anxiety, worry and fear. Yet, we all yearn for peace, joy, hope, love, and faith in the midst of these storms and we wonder how to achieve it.

Understanding these promises of Jesus, which Linda and I will discuss throughout the book, will benefit our lives on this Earth as well as ultimately determine where we spend eternity. There is abundant life waiting for each of us if we will reach out and grab it.

This book is about discovering the reality, purpose and blessings of our Lord's promises.

For over two decades, my wife, Linda, and I have traveled North America giving in excess of 500 parish retreats, workshops, seminars and conferences. We have been blessed to see our Lord do miracles in the lives of His children. It is a privilege to be used as an instrument of God.

We are Christians in the Catholic tradition. We were married in April of 1970 and God has blessed us with two beautiful daughters and four amazing grandchildren.

Our approach to God and church has always been very practical and down to earth. We believe that when we can take God and church and connect them to our everyday lives, at that point God and church will become real and meaningful. We have never written, preached or taught on anything that we haven't lived or are currently living.

There is often the thinking by many people that those in ministry have it all together. Let me correct that misconception as it relates to Linda and me. Quite frequently, we are hurting, broken and wounded people in need of the love, mercy, compassion, forgiveness and healing of Jesus. If, as evangelizers, we insist on waiting until our lives and church communities are in perfect spiritual condition, with all Christians living in perfect harmony, we would never do anything.

We must remember that Jesus did not establish His church for saints, but for sinners, people like you and me who strive for holiness, yet know the spirit is willing but the flesh is weak. For years, Linda and I have tried to accept this humbling reality. We work with whatever there is to work with and leave the outcome in God's hands.

As a Christian family, we can help one another by giving encouragement. I used to be a long-distance runner. I remember as I neared the end of a long race, my legs ached, my throat burned and my whole body would cry out for me to stop. This is when my teammates were most valuable. Their encouragement helped me push through the pain and finish the race.

Linda has always been that encouragement for me. In the same way, we as Christians can encourage each other. A kind word offered at the right moment can be the difference between continuing our call from God or quitting before we have achieved our potential and purpose.

Approach each day, striving to live the great commission of Jesus. Embrace the task with the firm conviction that you have something of value to share with others. Believe that you have the ability to enrich the lives of others and that you are indeed God's messenger and a resurrected person.

Believe that you are a unique masterpiece of God. In all the world there is nobody just like you. Nobody has your smile, your eyes or your voice. You are the only one in creation that has your set of abilities. That unique combination of gifts and talents is like a symphony. You are rare and in rarity there is great value.

Please begin to see that God made you for a unique purpose. God has a special job for you to do and no one else can accomplish that.

Many years ago, Linda and I embraced some powerful words from St. Paul.

"Preach the Word, whether convenient or inconvenient," he said. "Correct, rebuke and encourage others with great patience and careful instruction. For the time will come, when people will not put up with sound doctrine. They will turn their ears away from the truth and turn aside to false teachings. But you, keep your head in all situations, endure hardship, do the work of an evangelist, fulfill your ministry." 2 Timothy 4: 2-5.

These are strong words from the Apostle Paul. He is telling us that the time has come to seize the moment. God has put out a call to all of us. We are being asked to grow into a new and deeper intimacy with Jesus Christ.

What kind of a commitment is God asking of us as His children?

I believe that He is asking us to entrust everything, our lives, families, jobs and possessions, to His guidance and control. He wants us to believe that He can take care of us far better than we can take care of ourselves. It's time to take a stand for Jesus Christ and be the people of God that He is calling us to be. Allow Jesus to be the Lord of every part of our lives.

Can you imagine what would happen if every Christian would live by what they say they believe, seizing those opportunities to live by their faith in their families, marriages, jobs, churches and communities?

If we walk with Christ, He will change our character, clarify our values, modify our convictions and instill a sense of great integrity. He will also give our lives purpose, security, peace, courage and joy. Part of the Good News of Jesus Christ is that those around us will be the beneficiaries of God's work within us.

The challenge for each of us is whether we will recognize it, respond in obedience to God, and trust in His ability to work through us to fulfill His purpose.

On the cross, Jesus confronted His enemies, not with the power at His disposal, but with His unconditional love. It symbolized His servant's heart, not using the love of power, but the power of love, the kind of love that builds bridges, affirms people, and turns houses into homes.

The true position of leadership is not in an ivory tower, but on our knees before God, humbly seeking His mercy, love, grace, and forgiveness.

Pope Paul VI told us in his encyclical, "Evangelization in the Modern World," that the "Gospel message is not an optional contribution for the Church. It is truth. It merits having the apostle (that's us) consecrate to it all their time and all their energies, and to sacrifice for it, if necessary, their own lives."

When we started our ministry of sharing the Good News of Jesus Christ, we understood that we might never be asked to sacrifice our lives. However, we had to ask ourselves, what price are we willing to pay to spread the Good News by sharing our stories of faith? When each of us answers that question in our own lives, that's where the rubber meets the road.

It took Linda and me nearly 40 years to understand and live a very basic spiritual principle. While we are on this Earth, and none of us know how long we are going to be here, we are supposed to be in a relationship and partnership with our Lord Jesus Christ.

Now Jesus will always do what He promised. But, sometimes we find ourselves in situations that make us wonder how did we ever get here? We sometimes find ourselves going down a road that will only bring pain and heartache and we can't seem to find the exit ramp. The reason this often occurs is that we don't do what we are supposed to do in this partnership and relationship with Jesus Christ.

Many years ago, a very wise spiritual man told me that a person can miss the Kingdom of God by 18 inches. That's the average distance between a person's mind and his heart. Everyone reading this book will have some kind of definition and understanding of who they believe Jesus Christ is and what His Kingdom is all about. That is important and necessary in our spiritual development. However, the danger is that once we have arrived at that definition we lock it in and leave it in our heads. It is only when we invite Jesus Christ into our hearts that He can begin to reveal who He is and the true purpose of His kingdom.

Jesus often used parables to describe a spiritual or moral principle. I believe that His parables were and still are today "spiritual brainteasers."

For over two thousand years, Jesus has been asking us to think outside of the box, to rethink some of our common perceptions, to have a change of mind and a change of heart.

No matter who we are or where we are on our spiritual journey, we are called to have our mind, heart and thoughts radically changed by the Gospel of Jesus Christ.

It is our hope that as you read the words and ponder the thoughts of this book, whether for the first time or in a new and deeper way, you will invite Jesus into your heart.

I believe that Jesus Christ intended the Christian life to be much more than most Christians ever experience. Why is that?

This is not a judgment of anyone, but in ministering to well over 100,000 people over more than 20 years, Linda and I have personally seen and experienced evidence that many Christians are not aware of the spiritual power tools that are available to them every day. For nearly 40 years, we, too, were those Christians.

This book is about helping all of us identify what those tools are and how to effectively use them so we will have the abundant and blessed life that Jesus Christ came to give us, not just in Heaven but here on earth as well.

Linda and I believe that we are at a critical point in salvation history. We are all aware of the enormous problems in the world today. Pope Francis is telling us that if there was ever a time when the world needed to listen and respond to the messages of Jesus Christ, the present moment is that time.

As Christians, we must be willing to stand together and say, "Enough is enough!"

Doctors need medicine before they can heal. Cooks need ingredients before they can prepare a meal. Farmers need seeds before they can reap a harvest. The world needs Jesus before it can find answers to our problems and needs.

We live in a world filled with stress and anxiety. The world tries to convince you and me that believing in Jesus and His Gospel is all a lie and a waste of time.

Each of us has been given only so much time to live. Tens of thousands of people die each day without hearing about Jesus Christ. With so many people in the world waiting to be evangelized, we have to run hard and run to win.

You and I are the instruments of God's saving actions in the world today.

Many people are already allowing God to use them as His instruments and the music sounds wonderful. It happens when parents share the Gospel values with their children by what they say and then back it up with how they live their lives.

It happens when a nurse comforts a fearful patient or a youth minister takes the time to listen to the needs and problems of a teenager. It happens when we allow God to use us to reach out to someone in physical, emotional or spiritual pain.

In other words, it depends on our daily loving service to those around us. We don't have to be a scripture scholar or have a master's degree in theology to be a mediator of God's love and goodness. If that was a requirement for evangelizing, all of the Apostles would never have made the first cut for joining Christ's team.

Jesus preached powerfully and eloquently, but He also communicated God's love to the world by serving, healing, defending the oppressed, and laying down His life in love.

I recall that many years ago we were asked to visit a 34-year-old woman who had been in a wheelchair most of her life. She was poor, uneducated (at least by society's standards) and was in great pain. A debilitating physical disease had consumed her body.

When we arrived, she asked us to kneel down next to her. To our amazement, she began to pray for us that God would use us in a mighty way. When we looked into her eyes, Linda and I realized that we were seeing the face of Jesus. This woman had every right to be angry, sad, bitter, and unforgiving. But, through her brokenness she made the decision to be an instrument of God. We left that day knowing that, through her, we had been touched and changed by Jesus Christ.

So in the midst of all the obstacles, roadblocks and difficulties you face each day, your pain, brokenness, anger, sadness and at times unforgiveness, how do you live the life that our Lord Jesus is asking you to live? How do you live a life that touches and changes those around you with the love of Christ?

Linda and I truly believe that by deciding to read this book, you are well on your way to doing just that - building a strong spiritual foundation in Jesus Christ.

Enjoy the journey!

Deacon Glenn and Linda Harmon

Chapter 1

Building A Strong Foundation

Building a strong spiritual foundation on the teachings of Jesus Christ begins by looking at different ways you can strengthen, deepen and anchor your relationship with almighty God.

All that God requires is that you read these pages with an open mind and an open heart. If you will do that, if you will say in your heart and really mean it, "Lord, I am willing to receive whatever blessings, graces and spiritual awareness you have for me," then God will do wonderful things in your life.

You see, God is going to be planting spiritual seeds in your heart as you read every page of this book, because He knows exactly what you need at this moment in your life. Written words can be very powerful, especially when they reveal God's love for you and His plans for your life.

I know from my own experiences, and from the experiences of people who have attended our missions and retreats, that some of those seeds that God plants will bear fruit and blossom as you absorb the lessons in these pages. Some of those seeds may lay dormant for weeks, months or maybe even years, but God will bring them to blossom and bear fruit when He knows the time is right for you.

That's why, as you read these pages, we pray that you will look at each one as part of a journey of faith, a sort of pilgrimage on paper. And, as you go on this pilgrimage, we want you to realize that our Lord Jesus Christ will be with you every step of the way. He will be with you to rejoice in the good times and to support you in the difficult times.

Having presented our missions since 1992 all over the United States and Canada, one thing has become very evident to us. Like the people who come to our missions, we think that people who want to read our book will generally be in one of three places in their lives.

Some will be in what we call a resurrection moment in their lives. At this moment, everything is just great. God is pouring out His blessings, you can feel the presence of the amazing graces of God and you're just happy to be alive.

When we are in one of those moments, we just want to wrap ourselves in it because it feels so good. If that's where you are, you are likely reading this book because you want to find ways to keep this resurrection moment going in your life.

Others may be reading this because even though life isn't really bad for you right now you still know there is something missing. You may not know what it is, but there's a void, a hole. I'm hoping that in the pages of this book God will help you understand what is missing in your life and then help you to fill up that "empty" hole.

Finally, some of you are reading this because of something that might have happened in your past that you still haven't dealt with, or something that is going on right now. You're broken, you're wounded and you're hurting. You are very much in need of the healing touch of God.

No matter what is bothering you, or even if you feel you are doing fine but just want to continue on that same closeness with your Creator, it will always help to encourage you to remember that Jesus is the divine healer, the supreme physician.

If Jesus Christ can raise Lazarus from the dead and turn water into wine, He can certainly take care of any problems that we have in our lives, but we must be willing to accept what God has in store for us.

To do that, take a moment or two at any time while you're reading this book, or reflecting on the words you've read, and ask the Lord to open your mind so that you may experience and understand Him better in rewarding and insightful new ways.

Also, ask our Lord to soften your heart so that you can feel His presence. Then He can reach those areas of your heart that are desperately in need of His healing touch. Ask our Lord and

Savior Jesus Christ to hear your prayers, petitions and the desires of your heart, knowing that He is listening.

Perhaps it will help if you reflect again on the three questions that take each of us right to the core of our spiritual foundation.

First, do you believe, at this moment in your life, without any doubt, with no hesitation, that Jesus Christ is really who He says He is? Many people believe that He was a rabbi, a teacher, a holy man or a prophet. But, they don't believe He came into our world as the Messiah. This question has been at the root of our understanding of Jesus for more than 2,000 years.

Even in scripture, Jesus looked at the apostles and asked them, "who do people say that I am?" After the apostles tell Jesus all the titles, all of the labels that the people have given Him, He looks again at those same apostles and asks, "Who do you say that I am?"

You see, when it comes right down to the core of our spiritual reality, it doesn't make any difference what anybody else says about Jesus. What is important is who you and I, in the depths of our heart and our spirit, say that Jesus Christ is. Do you believe that He is the Messiah, the Christ, the savior of the world, your savior?

The second question is related to the first.

Do you believe that the promises of Jesus Christ are true?

As we begin to study scripture, reading and discussing the promises of Jesus Christ, we begin to realize how absurd His promises are to the world.

In much of our society in America, and in many other countries, people believe the promises of Christ are ridiculous. Do we accept the mindset of our society or are we going to wrap our hearts and minds around the promises of Christ? If you don't believe that Jesus is the Messiah, then there is no reason to believe that His promises are true. But, if you believe that Jesus is your savior then it becomes paramount in our lives that we believe His promises are true.

Beyond that, we must still address that third question. Are the promises of Jesus Christ for you? I know of many people who are willing to say "yes" to the first question and even to the second. But, this last one, they just can't buy. Why not?

One reason is because they may have a poor self-image. They look at themselves and remember how, throughout their lives, they have rejected, turned their back on and refused to have anything to do with Jesus Christ. And, because of that they don't believe that Jesus would offer His promises to them. They refuse to understand that's exactly the reason that Jesus went to the cross, was crucified and died - all for that person who is a sinner.

Those three questions are going to continue to be the common thread that runs through this entire book. Answers to those questions will tell you where your spiritual foundation is grounded and rooted.

How do I know that the answers to those three questions are essential for revealing where you're placing God in your life? How do I know that your answers also reveal your relationship to Jesus Christ and how you are welcoming Him into your life to help you or guide you - or not? Because I have been there myself.

You see, for the first 35 years of my life, if you asked me those three questions I would have told you that I believe in Jesus Christ and I believe in my Catholic faith. I would have no problem professing that with my mouth. But, if you saw how I lived my life, you would see that my actions did not match those words.

If you witnessed how I treated my wife, Linda, how I treated my two daughters, Christina and Kelly, and how I spent most of my days and most of my life it would clearly show that my words and actions did not match up to how I answered those questions.

If you want to know how deeply rooted your foundation is in Jesus, ask yourself what has happened to you when the going gets rough. For example, how have you reacted when a tragedy has taken place? Do you fall apart, do you crumble, do you almost vaporize? Or, in the midst of that tragedy, are you able to have a peace and hope that goes beyond all understanding?

As Christian people we are Easter people. We are to be people of hope when there is no hope. We are supposed to be people of joy when there is sadness all around us. When everybody around us is filled with fear, we are supposed to be people of faith, living in a society that is riddled with hopelessness, sadness, despair and tremendous anxiety.

I hear so many people say, "Glenn, if I could just be rid of all of my problems, and all of my anxieties, then I would have peace."

If that's your criteria for peace, you'll never get it.

Peace is not an absence of conflicts or problems. We will always have problems on this earth. But peace, true peace, the peace of Christ, is being able to deal with and respond to these problems with an inner peace that cannot be explained because it is not of human origin. It is Divine.

If you look at Jesus and the apostles, their lives were filled with troubles, problems and conflicts.

People were running them out of town. They were beating them. They were trying to kill them. Jesus had a lot of challenging problems. But, in the midst of all of that, He and His followers traveled from town to town and lived day to day doing just what He and His disciples were called to do - spread the Good News. You see, their hope was in Jesus. When your hope is in Jesus there's no reason to have anything else but peace.

Now, let's take that thought to the next level. If you are truly going to build our foundation on Jesus, then we must be willing to surrender all of these things - anxieties, fears, doubts and all the problems and challenges in our life - to the will of God.

Now, that sounds easy enough by saying it, but as human beings we love to have control of our lives. Or, we like to think we have control of our lives. Right now, as you're reading these words, your heart is beating, your lungs are breathing in oxygen. Do you realize that you have no control over that?

The only reason your heart is beating, the only reason your lungs are taking in air is that God wants it to work that way. You have no control over your heart beating. Every morning, when I wake up and realize my heart is beating, I say, "Oh, Lord, thank you for giving me another day."

We're all alive at this moment because God wants it that way. There are people who woke up this morning thinking they would have another day and yet they never live to see the end of their day. We don't have any control no matter how we try to live by our own will. It is God's will that is ultimately going to be fulfilled.

So, if we truly want to do God's will in our lives, which is to ground and root our spiritual foundation in His teachings, we need to surrender our will, our desires, our hopes and our dreams to Him. That's very hard for us when we live in a world that professes and promotes a philosophy that tells us to go get it, grab it, take it, hold on to it, and once you've got it, never let it go.

We are brainwashed throughout our lives with that mentality. That's the doctrine of the world. But, in the midst of that daily brainwashing by our society, Jesus Christ is telling us to give it up, surrender it, let it go. The loud messages we hear every hour of the day, in one form or another, are the world's messages - grab it, get it, hold on to it. Even with all that commotion filling our minds, sometimes we hear the small, still voice of our Lord Jesus Christ whispering, "Give it to me." What's surprising to us is that when we let it all go we find peace.

Now, please understand that when we surrender whatever areas of our life that we need to surrender, that does not mean that we surrender our responsibilities. For example, if you have a marriage that's not working the way you want it to work, wouldn't you say, "Oh, God, I will surrender my troubled marriage to you. I'm going to ask you to step in Lord. I'm giving you permission. I'm giving you control to step in and heal and bless this marriage."

That doesn't mean that you are not supposed to do everything you can yourself every minute of the day to make it a better marriage. God will do His part, you can be assured of that. However, you must also do your part in whatever area of your life you're surrendering.

You know, as I do, that this whole thing about our wills has been a problem since the beginning of time. When God created Adam and Eve, He looked at them and said, "Everything you can see, for as far as you can see, I'm giving it to you. It's yours. Enjoy it. Have fun with it, use it, benefit from it."

And then, as God looked at Adam and Eve, He pointed nearby and told them, "You can have everything except that little tree over there. You cannot have that. I don't want you to touch that tree."

That was God's will for Adam and Eve. We all know what happened. Adam and Eve decided that their will was better, that their will superseded God's will. Well, we've all been paying for that ever since.

This is a good time for you to pick up your Bible, the inspired Word of God, and read some scriptures that relate to this topic. Please read Genesis 3:1-19. I think it's very important, even critical, that we're able to locate helpful scripture passages like this in our Bibles so that we can highlight them or add some of our own thoughts.

The first scripture about Adam and Eve shows us what can happen when we refuse to be obedient to whatever God is asking us to surrender.

Now, please turn to the writing of Luke, Chapter 18, verses 18-23.

I'm sure you've heard this scripture since you were a little kid. You may, in fact, be very familiar with these words. So, I want to caution you. Don't let its familiarity steal the freshness of what God is about to say to you. Quite often, at least in my life, I know, when the priest, deacon or lector begins to read a particular scripture, something in my mind says, "Oh, yeah, I've heard that before." So, I begin to think of other things, as if God could tell me nothing new in the hundred and first time I've heard this scripture. However, that's when you miss the blessings God is offering you. He really wants your full attention.

I believe that God is going to tell you something very important in Luke 18, right now, as you read these words. Luke begins speaking about a "rich official."

Now, let me stop you right there. You see, those two words at the very beginning of this scripture should immediately tell us something important that sets the stage for what is to come. First of all, you know that he was rich, which meant he had money and he had possessions. He lived very comfortably and being a rich official meant he was a high-ranking person. He had a lot of power, authority and control. In other words, this rich official had everything his society of some 2,000 years ago told him he needed to be happy.

I'm sure you realize, looking at our own time in history, that nothing has really changed. The society we live in today is telling all of us the same thing. If you have a sufficient amount of money, possessions, power, authority and recognition you're going to be happy. You don't need anything else.

That's the biggest lie that the world tries to get us to believe. Unfortunately, most people buy into it. I used to be one of those people.

Well, if that is true then why did that rich official, with everything he had, search out and find Jesus?

It's very simple. It's because everything he had was not enough. He knew that something was missing. There was a hole inside of him. I call it a "God hole," and he was trying to fill that "God hole" with everything but God. And, it wasn't getting filled.

Each one of us has a God hole. We have been created by God with this hole inside of us. He knows that it is only going to be filled by God himself. But we run around spending most of our lives trying to fill it with everything else. Then, we wonder why it never gets filled. It's because God is the only one who's going to fill it, and He's the only one who's going to keep it filled.

Next, the rich official asked Jesus this question. Now get ready for this life changing question.

"Good teacher, what must I do to inherit eternal life?"

Wow!

Isn't that the ultimate question? Isn't that the "million dollar" question? Isn't that just what we all want to know?

Jesus, how can I be assured of spending an eternity with you?

As simple as that question is, it takes a tremendous amount of courage to ask Jesus that question.

Today, as you're reading this, are you prepared to ask Jesus that question" Be careful if you say, "Yes!"

If you think you're ready to say, "Lord, what do I have to do to have eternal life?" you'd better be prepared for the answer.

So often, in fact, people refuse to ask that question because they're afraid God might ask them to do something they don't want to do. God might tell them to surrender something, to let go of something that they don't want to let go of. Therefore, they never ask that question.

But, those same people will still say, "Oh, yes, Lord, you are my Savior." Basically, Jesus is their Savior as long as Jesus doesn't tell them to do anything they don't want to do.

So, it took a tremendous amount of faith for this rich official to seek out Jesus and ask Him this question. Jesus answered him, but first Jesus asked him, "Why do you call me good. No one is good but God alone."

So Jesus was coming back at this guy basically asking, "Are you saying that you believe that I am God?" That's a very interesting question. Jesus was testing this rich official, saying, "Do you really believe that's who I am?"

Jesus goes on to remind him, "You know the commandments. You shall not commit adultery, you shall not kill, you shall not steal, you shall not bear false witness and you shall honor your father and your mother.'

"I have observed these commandments since my youth," the rich official replied.

Now, that tells me a lot about this man. Jesus goes through every commandment and the official boasts, "Jesus, I've done all of these things."

Basically, this was a good man. He was a man who took all of these commandments seriously. At this point, I think the rich official thought he was off the hook. Of course, none of us will ever be 100 percent off the hook because we're healing, we're weak and we're sinful. So as good as we're doing, or as good as we think we are responding to the call of God, we will never be complete without accepting God's will.

That's why Jesus told the rich official that even though He was pleased that the man had done well in living out those commandments, "there is one thing left for you to do ... sell all that you have and distribute it to the poor, and you will have treasure in heaven ... then come, follow me," Jesus said.

Unfortunately, when the rich official heard this, he became quite sad, for he was very rich.

This scripture amazes me. This man got up the courage to ask Jesus this ultimate question, Jesus told him what he had to do and he refused to do it. You see, Jesus knew that money and possessions were getting in the way of this man building his spiritual foundation. Even though he knew and kept God's commandments, this rich official had made money and possessions his "god."

In the first commandment, God said, "I am the Lord, your God. You shall have no other gods besides me." This rich official thought he had been fulfilling all of God's commandments, but Jesus told him he was not fulfilling the very first one. Money and power had become his god, with a little "g," in place of God, with a big "G."

I'll telling you, nothing has changed in over 2,000 years. Today, people still have their little gods, with a little "g," that they place between them and the one true God.

If we had the opportunity, faith and courage to ask Jesus the same question that the "rich official" asked 2,000 years ago, Jesus would say the same thing to you and to me.

There is one thing left for you to do. Do you know what that one thing is that Jesus is asking you to let go of? I don't know what it is for you, but every time I have had the faith and courage to ask God that question, He always tells me, there's one more thing left for me to do - surrender.

This next scripture passage is one of my favorites in the New Testament. I invite you to read the Gospel of Mark, Chapter 10, verses 46-52.

Bartimaeus was not only blind but he was a beggar. This was his occupation, what he did for a living. Every morning, he would find a dusty road where people were passing by, spread out his cloak, sit down and beg for money.

Then, one day, to Bartimaeus' surprise, here comes Jesus Christ passing his way. I am not sure if he completely knew at this point who Jesus really was, but at least he knew He was a person of importance. Bartimaeus was so excited that he started screaming out to Him, hoping to get the attention of Jesus. His screaming annoyed and embarrassed the people around him and they tried to shut him up, but he would not be silent. Have you every noticed that when you try to talk about Jesus, so many people just want you to be quiet?

At that point, Jesus hears the cry of Bartimaeus and calls him over. The miracle that is always talked about in this scripture is that Jesus restores his sight. But for the miracle to occur, Bartimaeus had to do two profound things.

As with many poor beggars, the most important possession that Bartimaeus owned was his cloak. It was his office in the day time and what he wrapped himself in at night to sleep. When Jesus called to him, he had to make a life-changing decision.

He could have said to Jesus, "Wait a minute!" while he folded up his cloak and grabbed his alms from the crowd around him. But, the scripture says, "He threw aside his cloak." That was the most important possession Bartimaeus owned and he simply walked away from it, surrendered it, and let it go so he could meet Jesus.

At this point in your life, what is the one thing that you must surrender, really let go of and walk away from so you can have a life-changing encounter with Christ?

Now, remember that Bartimaeus was unaware that Jesus would be passing by that day. So when he finally found himself standing before Jesus, the Savior of the World, his Savior, he had no idea that Jesus would ask him the most important question he would ever hear.

"What do you want me to do for you?" Jesus asked gently.

Bartimaeus could have said, "I have no idea, can I get back to you tomorrow on this?"

But, obviously, he had given a lot of thought to what he wanted most in this world. So when Jesus asked that question, Bartimaeus immediately told him, "Master, I want to see." At that moment Jesus honored the desire of Bartimaeus' heart and restored his sight. Bartimaeus' life would never be the same again.

At this moment in your life, what is the deepest desire of your heart? What is that prayer that lies deep within you? If Jesus was to ask you the same question He asked Bartimaeus, "What do you want me to do for you?", what would be your answer?

I believe that Jesus also desires to work a miracle in your life. However, two things must occur before that miracle can take place. The first is to identify and surrender, let go of and walk away from whatever is preventing you from having a closer, personal and intimate encounter with Jesus Christ.

Maybe it's regret, guilt and shame about your past, a fear of the unknown of the future, low self-esteem or some sin that has gripped you and paralyzed you - perhaps anger, bitterness or unforgiveness. We all have something!!

Secondly, for a miracle to occur, it's important and necessary that you know the answer to the question that Jesus has been asking people for more than 2,000 years. "What is it that I can do for you?"

You can either be that person - like the rich official - who walks away sadly because you won't surrender that which you know you must give up, or you can be like Bartimaeus, who was obedient to Jesus Christ and received a miracle!

I Know Surrendering
Would Make My Life Better

Deep in my heart, I know if I surrender what God is asking me to let go of that my life will be better, because God is asking me to give up these things, to surrender these things, to give up control, simply because He loves me. If God didn't love me, He wouldn't care. He wants us to have a foundation that is deeply anchored and rooted in His will for our lives, not our will.

I encourage you to be aware as you read this book that God may ask you to surrender. If so, you must truly believe that God is who He says He is, then make the decision to let it go.

Another important topic that a lot of people struggle with is finding God in the ordinary everyday situations of our lives. I believe that God's love is revealed in the ordinary, everyday simple surroundings of our lives. Every person, situation and circumstance of our lives reveals God's love and God's will for us in some way.

True, it's easier to find God at a mission or a retreat because we know He will be there. It's easier to find God at church on Sunday when we're gathered with our faith community, when we're listening to beautiful music or when we're hearing the word of God preached.

Is it easy for you to discover God in the ordinary moments of your life on Tuesday morning at 10 a.m. or Thursday afternoon at 3 p.m., when life seems to be falling apart or life just seems to be ordinary and boring? I'm a firm believer that if we can not, or will not, search out and discover God in the ordinary times of our lives then we're going to miss God's presence most of the time.

There are even people who have come to our parish missions, in their own church, who are asking the same question, "Where is God?"

Often, something is going on in their life that troubles them or challenges them and they're wondering where God could possibly be in that situation.

I would never ask you to search out and look for God in your everyday lives, activities and situations if Linda and I weren't doing that ourselves, and benefiting from it. When we started this ministry, God made it very clear to us, in so many ways, that we were not to preach or teach on anything that we hadn't lived or experienced ourselves. We never have, and we never will.

So, we want to share with you in these pages, some of these times in the ordinary living or our lives when we thought that God had abandoned us and our family. We felt God just couldn't possibly be present in certain situations. Yet God revealed to us that He is truly God and truly present with us in every situation.

I grew up with two very beautiful parents. My Mom was an absolutely wonderful woman, a Catholic Christian lady who was strong in her faith.

When I look back over my life, I tell you there are a lot of things I've done that caused me to wonder if I should be doing missions, retreats and writing books focused on God. I survived because my Mom prayed me through a lot of stuff, both as a youth and as an adult.

Back in 1975, my Mom went to the doctor for a routine checkup and in the midst of that checkup the doctor discovered something that concerned him. He suggested that she have additional tests done. Well, she agreed to the tests and after a few weeks the doctor informed my mother that she had cancer.

Back in 1975 doctors didn't have the medical breakthroughs and treatments that they have now.

So, Mom began to go through her regular treatments, including chemotherapy and whatever else they did in 1975. As my mother was struggling with her cancer, I was deeply immersed in corporate America. I was truly the modern day "rich official" from the Bible.

I sought after money, power, recognition and authority. I was working 70, 80, 90 hours a week going after those things. My relationship with God was giving Him an hour a week and the rest of the week I was doing other things. You see, my spiritual foundation at that time was built on everything else except Jesus Christ and my Catholic church.

By the time 1980 rolled around, my Mom was experiencing some good moments but it was very obvious that she was getting worse. The cancer was definitely getting the best of her.

My Mom was a very holy woman. She prayed the rosary every day. I don't think I ever saw her miss a day. She always went to church, and had a deep love for the Eucharist.

I'd visit her periodically, but I didn't spend a lot of time thinking of her because I was too busy. However, when I did think of her, or visit her and sit by her, I remember thinking, how could God let this happen to a woman like my mother, this faith-filled, prayerful Christian woman. Why wouldn't God do something about this?

Meanwhile, I had been working for a promotion for a long time in this company I worked for and in December 1980, about a week before Christmas, I got a call from the national sales director.

"Glenn," he said, "you know that promotion you've wanted? Well, we're going to give it to you."

Well, I was elated.

Then, he said, "There's just one catch. You're going to have to move from San Diego, California, to San Antonio, Texas." I didn't even blink before I said, "I'll do it!"

In January 1981, a moving truck came to our house and loaded up everything we owned and headed toward San Antonio.

I remember going over and seeing my mother and breaking the news to her.

She started to cry. You see, I was an only child, her only son, and at this difficult time in her life, and my father's life, I was basically saying that money, power, possessions, recognition and authority were more important to me than she was. I was moving to pursue my corporate career.

Actually, our family was doing alright in San Diego. We had our two daughters, Christina and Kelly, a nice home, nice furniture and a couple of nice cars.

There was only one main reason I was leaving, I wanted that promotion and everything that went with it. And, I was even willing to leave my dying mother to get it. Now, it's not easy for me to tell you that. But, that's what I was doing. It humbles me to think how selfish I could be at times.

I remember when I said goodbye to my mother for the last time. She had this turban covering her head because she'd lost all of her hair during the illness. I gave her a hug and waved goodbye as she and my Dad stood on the porch, waving to me as I drove off to pursue my own plans.

It must have broken her heart to see her only son leave, particularly at a time like that. And it must have made it extremely difficult for my father, because he was left all alone to deal with my mother's illness.

After my family got situated in San Antonio, I'd call home every week or so to see how she was doing. The answer from my Dad was never good. When I talked to Mom on the phone, she'd try to put on a good face, try to be in good spirits. She'd ask how we were doing and I'd tell her. I know she was genuinely pleased, because all she ever wanted was for me to be happy. That's all mothers and fathers want, is for their children to be happy.

Several months later, I got a phone call from my Dad. When I heard his voice I knew that something was different. He said, "Glenn, your mother is worse. If you want to see her you better come home."

I got on an airplane the next day and flew to San Diego. As I was flying, I began to reflect on my life with my Mom and what a blessing she truly was to me.

Her favorite name for me, I recalled, was "Honey." It was always Honey this and Honey that. I was five years old before I realized my name was Glenn.

Before I would leave for school or before I went to bed at night, she would always say, "I love you, Honey."

You know, when you're five years old, or even 10 years old, you don't mind when your Mom calls you "Honey." But when you get to be a teenager, you may still want to hear the word "Honey," but you don't want to hear it from your Mom.

I'll never forget that time, I was probably 14 or 15 years old, and I was out in the front yard playing football with some of my buddies. It was time for dinner and my Mom opened the front door and called out, "Honey, it's time for dinner!"

Well, you can imagine the razzing I got from my buddies. I went into the house and said to my Mom, "I don't want you to ever call me Honey again."

And you know, she never did. That must have absolutely broken her heart.

After the plane landed, my Dad picked me up at the airport and drove me over to the hospital. We went right to my Mom's hospital room, but before we walked in my Dad stopped me and said, "Glenn, I have to tell you something. Your Mom will not recognize who you are. Your Mom has not said a word in over two months."

The cancer had gone to her brain. And my Mom, who was never very big in the first place, had gone down to 65 pounds.

"So don't be shocked," my Dad said. "She won't know who you are, she won't understand what you're saying and she will not be able to speak."

I walked in. I have to tell you I'm a big tough guy and I've seen a lot of things but it hit me pretty hard. My Mom was curled up in a little ball on the bed. I really didn't want to face this situation, and I felt angry. I didn't express my anger, but I was furious inside with God. I was thinking, "God, how could you do this?"

Now, for the last several years, I had two major prayers when it came to my Mom. First of all, I prayed that God would heal her. Over and over and over again I prayed that God would heal her.

Well, it didn't appear that God would heal her so I began praying that God would take her. He wouldn't heal her and He wouldn't take her, so I said, "Lord, what are you doing? You're certainly not answering any of MY prayers. So maybe you're not really who you say you are. Maybe you're really not that all powerful, all sovereign, almighty God."

Then, I walked over and sat down on my Mom's bed. I put my hand on her shoulder and I began to share with my Mom everything that I should have said to her when she could understand me.

Why do we do that? Why do we wait until so often it's too late? If you need to tell somebody you love them, don't wait another day. Tell them today! If you need to forgive somebody, or if you need to allow somebody to forgive you, don't wait another day because we are only guaranteed the present moment.

After about 20 minutes of sharing all of these feelings, words, and thoughts with my Mom, knowing that she couldn't hear me, that she didn't understand me, I finally got to the point where it was just too much.

I remember bending down and giving her a kiss on her forehead. Then I got up and started walking toward the door. I told my Dad I'd meet him out in the hall.

As I got to the door I heard this gasp behind me, and I knew the sound came from my father. I turned around and looked at my Dad. All of the blood had just drained from his face. He was white as a sheet, and he was staring at my Mom.

I turned toward the bed and saw my Mom, who was riddled with cancer. This wonderful, beautiful lady lifted up her head, looked at me and she said, "I love you, Honey."

You see, in the midst of what appeared to be an absolute tragedy, where I thought that God had abandoned me and my mother and my father, God was right in the middle of that situation. Right there!

And I believe He kept my Mom alive long enough so that I could hear those words, "I love you, Honey."

Today, those words ring as clear and as loud as they did back in 1982. You see, I learned that God is all powerful, God is sovereign, God is almighty.

Is It Time
To Re-evaluate Your Priorities?

When you have one of those moments when you believe God cannot possibly be in the situations of your life or you're even questioning whether God even exists and you're doubting His promises, God does know exactly what you need.

If you will allow Him into your mind and into your heart, if you will continue to search for our living God in all situations and in all things around you, He will help you to build and strengthen your spiritual foundation.

Our Closing Prayer

We Thank God
For His Graces In Our Lives

Lord, we thank you for your love, mercy, and amazing graces. Lord, we ask that you protect us, that you surround us with your holy and protective angels, that you wrap us, Lord, in your bubble of protection each day and night.

Lord, we know that you are the Savior of the world. We know, Lord, that you are the Messiah and the Christ. Lord, help us understand what that means for our own personal lives.

We ask this through the power of your Holy Spirit, that you help us to believe your promises and that we understand that they truly are for each and every one of us.

And we ask all of these prayers in your precious and holy name.

Amen.

Call To Action

1) What were your honest answers to those three questions?

2) At this moment in your life, where is your spiritual foundation built?

3) What miracle do you want Jesus to do in your life now?

4) What must you surrender in your life for that miracle to happen?

5) Where do you find God in your everyday life?

Chapter 2

Outsiders Need Not Apply

Have you ever felt rejected, misunderstood or unfairly judged? Ever felt like you could never forgive someone for how they treated you or how badly they made you feel? These are feelings that are common experiences for each of us. But, for some of us, these feelings are so deeply hurtful that they begin to incapacitate us, to change how we deal with other people. They are feelings that can ruin our lives, feelings that we don't know how to overcome.

The experiences I will share with you in this chapter may help you to break those chains of resentment, anger, rejection and unforgiveness that have been gripping you for much or even most of your life.

For many others, my messages may make you squirm in your chair because you'll realize you need to make changes in your life, in your views, or changes in how you treat other people. But, those will be changes for the better and help you build your spiritual foundation.

I can say this because when I first prepared this message for one of our missions, I discovered how much I had to change. I still remember how hard that was, but I'm also very glad I made those changes.

Changes such as how I approach other people, how I treat people in difficult circumstances and how I offer them mercy when they need it. Very simply, this chapter's theme is about mercy. It's about how we give mercy to others and how we receive mercy ourselves. You'll find this is a very revealing and very rewarding lesson.

When Saint John Paul II was giving one of his sermons about our spiritual journey on this Earth, he said that it begins at the moment of conception and it goes on until God calls us home.

He said our spiritual pilgrimage starts in our hearts, because we cannot give to anyone else what we do not have ourselves.

Earlier in these pages, I challenged all of us to see where our spiritual foundation is grounded and rooted. Is it grounded and rooted in the gospel of Jesus and the teachings of your church or is it grounded in the values of the world?

You need to first look into your heart. Our Holy Father tells us that the second step, after it begins in our hearts, is that it then extends to the believing community.

As believers in Jesus Christ, how do we treat one another?

When somebody does something that hurts us, for instance, there are three basic ways that we can respond - by revenge, by justice or by mercy.

Responding with mercy, however, isn't usually a choice you may think about making. Yet it can be a choice that is good for both you and the person you are forgiving.

As a Catholic Christian man, I thought I knew what mercy was. Then, as I began thinking and praying deeply about it, God showed me I had no real idea about the role mercy should play in our everyday lives.

As Catholics, we hear the word mercy in our Mass, in our liturgy. The word "mercy" is mentioned more than 240 times in the New Testament. When God chooses to mention a word or a theme 240 times, I believe He knows it's very, very important for us. God knows that because of our human, finite brain, He has to continue to mention mercy over and over again in different ways so that we will begin to understand the importance of it and how we can practice it more easily.

Rather than mercy, our first response to injustice or hurtful experiences is often revenge. Basically, revenge is rooted in history. There are multitudes of examples involving revenge throughout the Bible, from generation after generation.

You can see it in today's society and in your own life.

Simply put, revenge is giving somebody more than they gave you.

The second way to respond is with justice, the basis of our legal system of laws and courts. We hear a lot about justice. Justice is basically giving somebody a measured response that gives them pretty much what they gave to us. Revenge and justice are the two responses that you will hear from the world.

What we generally never hear from the world, and what we always hear from Jesus, is the third choice, mercy. The gospel of Jesus is all about mercy, which is giving someone what they don't deserve. Giving mercy to someone who has hurt, insulted, or rejected you is probably the last thing they would expect of you. In fact, it can often defuse a heated or emotional situation.

Have any of you ever prayed, "Oh God, give me what I deserve"?

Whether you realize it or not, I'm sure you weren't praying that.

Usually we pray, "Oh, Lord, give me your mercy." even though we are praying for something we do not deserve. When I reach the point in my prayer life where I am willing to ask God for mercy, how can I turn around and tell God I am not going to show another person mercy?

Throughout the Bible and throughout Church history, there are countless examples of mercy, freely given and freely received. Acts of mercy often changed lives, and even the world.

Mercy does not take money. Mercy does not require a great intellect. All mercy requires is an obedience to God and a compassionate heart.

As you read this, think about how wiling are you to be obedient to God and how compassionate is your heart?

Once again, I want to remind you that at one time in my life I thought I understood mercy and how it's used. However, I think that much of the misunderstanding that I used to have about mercy centers on perception.

Because many of us don't understand our perceptions of certain things, we wind up making false perceptions, which then become the basis for our actions.

Usually, our false perceptions involve opinions of what we perceive a person to be, and we respond to a person based on that perception of what we perceive them to be.

Evaluate Your Perceptions of People And Situations Carefully

Let me give you a very practical example of how misperceptions can cause an improper response.

In my diocese, I have a good friend who is a priest. One time, he was telling me about this story, a true story.

One Sunday morning, he was preparing for Mass and he was going to use incense. So prior to Mass he asked the altar server to begin to prepare the charcoal and incense for the service.

But the altar server did not tell the priest that he had never done that before. He just said, "Yes, Father," and the priest left the sacristy to take care of some other business.

Minutes later, the priest returned, put on his vestments and the Mass began.

Well, when it was time to incense the altar, the priest assumed that the altar server had prepared the charcoal, and that by now it was red-hot and ready to receive the incense.

He motioned to the altar server to bring the charcoal and incense to the altar. As he began to put the incense on the charcoal, he suddenly realized that the charcoal was ice cold.

Glancing at the altar server, he realized it was too late to do anything. He just put the incense on the charcoal, knowing nothing was going to happen. He continued to incense the altar but as soon as he did, 20 to 30 people in the congregation began to cough uncontrollably.

Why?

Because they thought there was incense burning and they always cough when there is incense. Believing they were seeing the priest incensing the altar, they began to cough. They responded according to their perception, rather than to what was really happening.

That illustrates one of our main struggles with mercy.

Our perception of the person and our perception of the situation versus the reality of the person and the reality and truth of the situation are often two different pictures.

Remember, if we want to understand the truth, not "a" truth, but the real truth about a particular situation it is important that we go to the master teacher, and that is Jesus.

In your Bible, turn to Luke's gospel, Chapter 17, beginning with verse 11. I'm urging you to do this because it's important that you realize that what you are about to read is the "living" word of God that is as important and relevant to our lives today as it was to the people of 2,000 years ago.

As you begin to read this passage, the living word of God, it is important that you think about what this scripture means to you. Don't imagine what this means to any other reader of this book, but only what does this passage mean to you, personally, in your life.

"As Jesus continued His journey to Jerusalem, He traveled through Samaria and Galilee. As He was entering a village, 10 lepers met Him. They stood some distance from Jesus and raised their voices, saying, 'Jesus, Master, have mercy on us.'

"And when He saw them, He said, 'Go show yourselves to the priest.' As they were going they were cleansed. And one of them, realizing he had been healed, returned, glorifying God in a loud voice. He fell at the feet of Jesus and thanked Him. He was a Samaritan."

Remember that word, Samaritan. That's very important in this scripture.

Jesus said to the crowd, "Ten were cleansed, were they not? Where are the other nine? Has none but this foreigner returned to give thanks to God?"

Then He said to the Samaritan, "Stand up and go. Your faith has saved you."

Now let's go back and look more closely at this scripture. Whenever we read scripture, our church encourages us to do several things. For instance, our church always encourages us to ask, "What does this scripture mean to me?"

We are also supposed to try to go back to the time in which the scripture was written to understand who the people were that God was speaking to and what the situation and the culture was at the time. If we can understand that to some degree, it will help us understand in a fuller sense what God is saying to us today through scripture.

As I began to reflect on this Bible passage, the first thing I did was to try to imagine myself as a leper, living 2,000 years ago.

Can you begin to imagine what that must have been like?

These 10 lepers did not wake up one morning and say, "Oh, God, give me leprosy!"

They didn't ask for leprosy. I'm sure they didn't want it, but they had it. Because they had leprosy, the people, society, and even the church of the time treated them as outcasts, alienated them and made them go live in caves away from their families. Lepers had to live together. People would bring food to them, while keeping their distance.

Can you imagine what that must have been like? The only difference between those lepers and you and me is that they had leprosy and we don't. They were husbands, wives, mothers, fathers, children, sisters and brothers. Since they had the disease of leprosy, the people of their day refused to show mercy to them.

At any time in your life, were you ever in a situation that you didn't cause, you didn't choose it to happen, but just because of the reality of the situation you were treated like a leper?

People alienated you and basically told you that you didn't belong here and to get out of the city! "If you want mercy," they said, "you'd better get it from God because you're not going to get it from us."

Those 10 lepers were in such desperate need of mercy that they broke the law of their society. They came within the city limits. That meant they were breaking the law. Have you ever needed mercy so badly that you were willing to do something, anything, to get it?

When the lepers saw Jesus passing by, they yelled out, "Jesus, Master, have mercy on us!"

Now, as a good Jew, and Jesus was a good Jew, He should have walked right by and not said a word. You see, good Jews were not supposed to talk to lepers.

If anyone came anywhere near a leper, the leper was supposed to scream out "Unclean! Unclean!" so that other people would know that they were getting too close to a leper.

How would you like to have to yell out, every time someone got close to you, "Unclean! Unclean!"

How would that touch your heart and your soul and what would that do to your self esteem?

Well, Jesus also broke the law because He spoke to these lepers.

What Jesus was trying to tell the people of His time, and what He's trying to tell us today, is that many times the spirit of the law outweighs the letter of the law.

The letter of the law was prohibiting talking to those lepers. The spirit of the law was reaching out and showing them mercy.

Jesus gives them instructions, telling them to go to see the priest.

As all 10 were leaving to find the priest, all of them were healed. Yet only one of them returned to thank Jesus.

So, Jesus questioned them on that.

"Weren't 10 cleansed? Where are the other nine?" He said.

Do You Remember To Thank God When Prayers Are Answered?

What that Bible scene reminded me is how often in my life I have asked God to do something for me. I have prayed to God, asking for something. God granted my prayer and I never even bothered to thank Him. For many years of my life, I never got on my knees and humbly thanked God, giving Him praise and glory for answering my prayer.

Has that ever happened to you? You have prayed and prayed and prayed, asking God to give you something, grant the desire of your heart, and He's done it. And you never bothered to say, "Thank you, Lord, for answering my prayer."

If you recall, I asked you to remember the word Samaritan.

To understand what I'm about to say, you need to know that the Jewish people had a very narrow concept of God. They also had a very narrow concept of the ministry of Jesus Christ.

For one thing, the Jewish people believed that God only loved the Jews. All foreigners, that is, anyone who wasn't Jewish, were second-class citizens.

So what Jesus was trying to point out to the people of the time is that even though this person was a Samaritan, Jesus healed the Samaritan. He showed mercy to the Samaritan because - unlike in the Jewish religion - the mercy of God has no boundaries. The mercy of God is available to anyone, at any place and at any time. We are all supposed to respond to one another in the same way, offering them our mercy, as Jesus does for us.

If we claim that we are a follower of Jesus Christ, our mercy should be available for anyone, in any place, at any time, inspired by Jesus' example.

If we do not believe that Jesus is the Messiah, if we do not believe the teachings of Jesus Christ, then we don't have to do it.

But, as Catholic Christians, every Sunday we come in to church, we stand and we proclaim our profession of our faith, which is that Jesus is Lord and we accept His teachings.

Have you ever felt rejected?

Have you ever felt alienated?

Have you ever felt like you just don't belong?

We all have at one time or another. But it is only when we begin to understand what it feels like to be rejected, when we do not receive the mercy we need from others, that we begin to say, "I don't ever want to do anything to make anyone else feel that way."

At this point, we begin to realize that the mercy of Christ has no boundaries. Since the beginning of time, human beings have erected boundaries, put up walls between themselves and others. The gospel of Jesus always calls on us to shatter any boundaries we have made.

Right now, in every one of our lives there are people that we need to show mercy to and we don't want to do it. Yet the gospel, this particular gospel of Jesus, is calling us to be more than we want to be, to think of others more than ourselves.

Each one of us reading this can think of at least one person that we know who is in desperate need of our mercy. Maybe it's a family member we're angry with and we've alienated them. Maybe it's somebody at work or maybe it's a neighbor or a friend. But there's always somebody that Jesus is asking us to show mercy to because He unconditionally shows mercy to us.

Now, we've been doing some heavy prodding here. We've been pushing, urging, nudging you to show forgiveness to others, to be more forgiving in your daily lives, to be more understanding and loving, as Christ is, as He urges all of us to be.

Rather than preaching to people, we are called to share our own experiences, our own problems and challenges, and share how Christ always helped us to overcome those challenges with His strength, His vision, and His forgiveness.

When Linda and I began this ministry, as apostles of Jesus Christ, He made it very clear to us that we were never to preach or teach on anything that we had not experienced or were presently experiencing in our lives.

Jesus Christ Leads Us And Challenges Us

I think it will help you to understand what we mean if I share an experience I had many years ago when Linda and I moved to Louisiana from southern California.

I was to start work for the Diocese of Lake Charles, Louisiana, as Director of Evangelization.

Now, keep in mind that I had spent over fifty years of my life in San Diego. That's where I was born, that's where I was raised, that's where I met and married my bride, Linda; that's where our two daughters were born and raised and that's where all of my friends were.

Everything that ever meant anything to me, everything that felt comfortable to me, was in southern California.

But Jesus made it very clear to Linda and me that we were to leave everything, home, adult children, a grandchild and friends in Southern California, and move to Lake Charles, Louisiana, where we didn't know a single person.

The early apostles, who traveled throughout many countries, probably felt much the same as we did when we arrived in Lake Charles. The culture was so different from what we were accustomed to that we felt like we had landed on the planet Mars.

In the first 30 days of working for the Diocese of Lake Charles, I made the decision that I was going to try to visit as many Catholic churches in the diocese as I possibly could. I simply wanted to introduce myself and ask the pastor and staff how I might be of service to them.

I didn't go in with any agenda or any special goals. I basically wanted to listen to people's views regarding evangelization. Altogether, I visited 26 or 27 Catholic churches in the diocese in 30 days.

At one parish, I'll never forget it, the pastor had gathered about 15 members of his staff together. We had about an hour and a half visit and shared all kinds of ideas. Basically, I just listened and learned.

When the meeting was beginning to wrap up, a white-haired gentleman who had not really said anything at all during the entire meeting, said, "Glenn, may I ask you a question?" I said, "Yes, you can."

He said, "How long do you expect to be here in Louisiana?"

I told him I knew without any shadow of a doubt that God had called me here, and I imagined that when God wanted us to leave He would make it as clear as possible.

"Well, however long that is," he told me, "however long you live here, don't ever expect to accomplish anything."

I kind of sat back, looked at him and asked him why he'd said that.

"Because you are an outsider," he said. "You don't look like us, you don't act like us, you don't talk like us and you certainly don't understand our spirituality. Have a nice day."

I looked at him and said, "Thank you ... Father."

As I prepared to leave that meeting and walked to my car, all kinds of emotions began to run through my head. I was angry. How dare this man say that to me. I was sad. I was confused. But the number one feeling that hit my heart was alienation. He had just dismissed all of my efforts and told me I didn't belong. I felt rejected. I was an outsider. I was alienated.

As I was driving back to my office, with tears running down my face, something hit me and I pulled over to the side of the road.

Sitting there, I cried out loud, "Oh, My God, My Lord, have I ever said anything, have I even done anything, to make anyone feel like I'm feeling right now? Lord, if I ever have (and I guess I knew I had), please forgive me."

You see, it's only when we begin to understand what it's like to feel alienated that we do not ever want to alienate others.

Thankfully, I thought that painful situation was over. But, it wasn't.

About two weeks later, during my morning prayer time, in His own very powerful way, God made it clear to me that I was to visit this Catholic priest, this pastor who had just told me that I didn't belong, that I was an outsider, that I would never have his blessing; and that I was to go and ask him to forgive me!

I remember thinking, "What?! Jesus, you have got to be kidding! You can't be serious!"

I did absolutely nothing to this man. Why should I ask him to forgive me?

Well, let me tell you, I struggled with that for a couple of weeks. But, as only God can do, He just kind of nudged me and coaxed me until finally I said, "OK, Lord, I don't agree with it, I don't understand it. I think you're wrong. But, if that's what you want me to do, I will go ask this man to forgive me."

Reluctantly, I called him and made an appointment. When I got there, his secretary let me in and as I walked into his office the pastor looked at his watch and said, "You have two minutes."

I thought to myself, "Lord, are you sure you want me to do this?"

Now, remember, there are three basic ways that we respond to people when they do something we don't like that's hurtful.

We can respond in revenge, which is grounded and rooted in hatred and bitterness. And, to be honest with you, I thought of a lot of ways I could get revenge.

Another way was justice. I was going to come back and tell this guy a couple of things that he probably didn't want to hear. Or I could treat him like HE was an outsider.

But, Jesus was telling me to give him something he didn't deserve - my mercy.

I sat down and I looked at him a moment, then I said, "Father, I am here to ask for your forgiveness."

He sat back in his chair and he looked at me.

"I must have done something to you," I said. "I must have, in some way that I don't know, done something to you that angered you for you to say what you said to me. I must have said or done something that hurt you or offended you. I am so sorry. Please forgive me."

Well, this pastor, who up to this point had been very brash and very arrogant, lowered his head and began to doodle on a piece of paper. For the next three or four minutes, he continued to face his desk and didn't look up once. He didn't say a word.

And, I didn't say another word.

After a few minutes of this I realized that he wasn't going to say anything.

Then, I politely remarked, "Excuse me, Father." I got up and left.

As I was walking out to my car, I said, "OK Lord, I did what you wanted. I asked him to forgive me and the man didn't even say a word. Lord, I am finished with this."

Well, I may have been finished but, you see, God wasn't finished with this situation at all.

A couple of weeks later, during my prayer time, God said to me that I was to call this pastor, this same pastor who called me an outsider, this pastor who wouldn't even accept my mercy and my forgiveness, and I was to ask him to do a workshop with me.

I said, "Lord, you have really got to be kidding!"

I didn't even want to be in the same city with this man and God was asking me to work hand in hand with him, to give a workshop together!

Well, this hard head of mine still couldn't figure out what Jesus was trying to do. I struggled, and struggled, and struggled, and finally one day, I called this priest and said, "I'm doing a workshop on the Holy Spirit in about a month and a half. Would you like to be a co-facilitator with me, a co-retreat master?"

To be honest with you, I expected the guy to hang up on me. Or, say "No, thank you."

What he said was, "I'll think about it."

Now, that shocked me.

Then, he hung up. I thought he'd think about it for about five seconds and I'd never hear from him again.

"Lord, I've done it," I said. "I'm not going to call him back."

Well, about three days later, I got a call back from this priest.

"I would like to do the workshop with you," he said. "You write what you want to write and I'll write what I want to write and we'll just get together and we'll do it."

"OK," I told him, "that's fine with me."

You know, of course, that the last thing I ever wanted to do was sit down and work with this guy.

The day of the workshop finally came and there were about 100 people at the retreat center and we presented that workshop. It was kind of a strange feeling. I had no idea what he was going to say and he had no idea what I was going to say.

But, as only God can manage to accomplish good things in situations like this, when we both came together for that presentation, it turned out that what we said together was powerful. It was, undeniably, an inspired movement of the Holy Spirit that just goes beyond all understanding.

I saw people's lives change that day at that retreat. Just imagine, God was using two men who couldn't stand each other, who didn't even want to be in the same room with each other - to change lives.

When the retreat was over, and people were getting ready to leave, I said, "Ladies and Gentlemen, thank you for coming. I would really like us to take a moment to thank Father."

Everybody applauded and said how wonderful the workshop was. About that time I was also going to leave, and was heading for the door when the priest stopped me.

"Glenn, would you wait a minute?" he said. "I just want to say publicly that I have said some very unfair, unjust, and untrue things about Glenn Harmon. I want you to know that in just the short amount of time that Glenn has been here I have come to realize that he's one of the greatest gifts that God has ever brought to this diocese."

Mercy!

Originally, I didn't want to have any part of this whole thing. But I made a choice to be obedient to God and to show mercy to somebody that I really didn't think deserved it.

Now I want to emphasize that I don't take credit for any of this. It's God who made this happen. But by my being obedient to God's call, the whole experience changed both our hearts.

That former Pastor is now a retired priest in the Lake Charles diocese and we absolutely have a great relationship together. You see what can happen when we begin to treat one another with mercy rather than justice, or revenge?

Who in your life is in desperate need of your mercy?

You see, when we begin to see people as God sees people, the reality of who those people are becomes apparent rather than our perception of who they are.

When Jesus chooses to show me mercy, every minute of every day, He doesn't see who I am, He sees who I could be, and His mercy is slowly transforming me from the inside out.

If 20 years ago anyone had ever told me that I'd be living the life I am living now, I'd have told them, "You're two cards short of a full deck! Your elevator doesn't go all the way to the top!"

But the mercy of God, the unconditional love and mercy of almighty God has transformed this hardheaded, bitter, resentful, vengeful man into a man who wants to be obedient to God above everything else. If that means I have to humble myself in the sight of the Lord, and ask somebody to forgive me or show mercy to somebody that I don't want to forgive, all I have to do is look at the body of our Lord hanging on a cross in every Catholic church in the world. Because that cross reminds me that I have hurt God far more in my life than anybody has ever hurt me.

I have reached a point in my life that there is absolutely no way that I can get on my knees and ask God for forgiveness and mercy, and then look at that same God and say, "I want your forgiveness and mercy but I will not show it to this person or this person or that person."

I just can't do that anymore.

God has made me aware of the difference between my perception of who a person is, versus the reality of who they really are. I'll never be the same.

Who's That Person Sitting Next to You?

The next time you're in church, or with any other group of people, turn around and look at the people behind you, maybe even at the sign of peace during a Mass. Then, look at the person beside you and in front of you.

Some of the people you know well, some you know only by name, others you don't know and have no idea who they are or what they're like.

I have realized from experience that if you know any of them long enough that with God's help you will develop a clear perception of the reality of who they are. You will come to an understanding of who they really are, and I believe you'll find they're not anything like you perceived them to be before you knew them.

When we begin to ignore our perception of a person and begin to see the reality of the person, how God sees them, it will become easier and easier to show them mercy, especially if you honestly believe they don't really deserve it.

Meeting The Poorest
Of The Poor

It may help you understand the importance of mercy in your life, and in others' lives, if I give you an example from my own life.

I'd like to tell you about one of the greatest acts of mercy I've even experienced. In a deeply profound way it changed my life forever.

The person who showed me that mercy, when I needed it most, has no idea what it really did for me; nor will this person ever know.

In San Diego, California, Linda and I were active in the Catholic church. If you know anything about San Diego geography, you probably know that it is just north of Tijuana, Mexico.

The Catholic church we belonged to was very much involved in helping to feed the poorest of the poor in Tijuana. Now, until this experience, I could never understand the difference between the poorest of the poor and, simply, the poor. I discovered there is a difference.

Once each month, parishioners would bring food staples to church and we would take the rice and the beans and all the other donations and put them in brown bags, each one with the same kinds of foods and the same amounts. We'd load all of the bags up and cross over the border to Tijuana and feed, literally, the poorest of the poor.

One particular Saturday, it was my responsibility to get all of these bags ready, to help load them into 10 or 12 trucks and then, when we arrived, to stand beside one of those trucks and give out our bags of food to those in need.

It was the responsibility of certain people across the border in Tijuana to decide who got the food. That wasn't our responsibility. So, on this trip, we drove across the border through Tijuana and down a narrow inland road to get to where they had planned the distribution point.

Some of the images I saw when we arrived were unbelievable. To understand the contrasts, look around your home, the dwelling you live in, with all its different rooms, all the possessions you have, and think about your yard and landscaping.

Now imagine that instead of crawling into a comfortable bed at night in your well protected, warm, dry home, you crawl into a cardboard box. And, your wife and children will all crawl into that cardboard box with you.

Because, that's where they all live, the poorest of the poor.

If it rains, your cardboard "house" will crumble around you and be washed away. In the morning, wet, cold and hungry, you and your family will begin the day looking for more cardboard boxes, ones that haven't already been found by another family. You secure it and erect it in some way and you start all over again setting up your household.

Now, here's another image to try to grasp. When we arrived at our distribution point, we saw a line of people that, honestly, extended so far that I could not see the end.

We were told that the people coming for the food we brought were handpicked from the poorest of the poor, and had been waiting in line for up to eight hours, often after walking for miles to be there.

At that moment, I began to realize that there was not enough food for all the people who would be coming, people who were tired, hungry, and weary from waiting for so long.

Once our trucks were parked, I began preparations for distributing the bags of food in my truck. All the other trucks were doing the same.

A person next to me told me how much we could give out to the crowd. Usually it was three bags per family, at the most. The person directing the distribution at my truck would say, as people came forward, "uno," "dos," "tres" - indicating one to three bags for each family.

Well, it didn't take me long to realize I was running out of food and there were still a lot of people there. After I gave out the last bag of food, my truck was empty. I turned around and looked at a woman who was standing behind the person who had gotten the last bag.

She was a mother with five little children. The oldest child was maybe 10 or 11. The others' ages ranged all the way down to two. They had all been in line for eight hours to get food just to sustain themselves for a while longer.

As I looked at her, I had to tell her "No mas," which, in Spanish, means "No more."

Then I braced myself.

Remember there are three ways you can respond to a person when they do something to you.

Justice, an eye for an eye, giving someone back exactly what they've given to you. Revenge, giving them something even worse than they've given to you. Or mercy, giving them something they don't really deserve.

It was hot. It was nearly noon. She had been waiting in line for hours with five little kids. This woman had every right to be angry and vengeful or at least to feel justified in trying to hurt me in some way, whatever she determined that to be. And that's what I was waiting for.

When she looked at me, I will never forget that beautiful lady's eyes, and what she said to me, "May God bless you!"

She took the hands of her little children, turned and they walked away. That profoundly changed my life. I watched her walk away with tears running down my face. Mercy is giving someone what they do not deserve. She gave me mercy!

Think about who, in your life, is desperately in need of your mercy.

The gospel of Jesus is not always easy to listen to and not easy to follow, because the gospel of Jesus Christ will always call us to be more than we want to be.

When we reach a point in our relationship with Jesus where we say, think or feel we're comfortable, when we tell our Lord, "Jesus, this is it, this is as far as I'm going, this is as much as I'm going to do," it's then that Jesus will call us out of our comfort zone.

Wherever you are in this whole topic of mercy, it's OK to be there, because that's where you are. It's just not OK to stay there.

Our Closing Prayer

May God bless you with every good gift. May He keep you pure and holy in His sight at all times.

May He bestow the riches of His grace upon you, bring you the Good News of salvation, and always fill you with love for all people.

Father, look kindly on your children who put their trust in you; bless them and keep them from all harm.

Help your people to rejoice in the mystery of redemption and to win its reward, eternal salvation.

We ask this in the name of Jesus Christ the Lord.

Call To Action

1) Has anyone ever made you feel like a leper? Have they ever made you feel as if you were an outsider, that you didn't belong or fit in? How did that experience make you feel?

2) Have you ever made someone else feel like a leper? How does it make you feel to know that you have the ability to treat others that way?

3) When you realize that Jesus offers and shows you mercy everyday, how does that touch your heart? How do you want to respond to Jesus?

4) Who are the people in your life right now who are in need of your mercy?

5) What specific ways can you be merciful to those people today?

Chapter 3

Walk By Faith

[Glenn Harmon: My wife, Linda, is a woman of faith and her words are powerful. She is the only person who has ever loved and forgiven me unconditionally. She lives what she believes, which is a rarity among people in today's world. In this chapter, she will offer you many "spiritual power tools" to assist you in building your spiritual foundation in Jesus Christ.]

By Linda Harmon

If you read our first book, **"Jesus, You Can't Be Serious?"**, this chapter will be familiar to you. But please read and enjoy it once again because most likely you are in a different place in many areas of your life now, so our Lord will give you new insights to ponder and use.

However, if this is your first reading of "Walk by Faith," know that countless women have approached me, telling me that my story of faith has set them free and put them on a new pathway of hope, joy, love, healing and faith.

They have verified what I also believe, that the words in this chapter can change your life forever. That's why Glenn and I made the decision to include "Walk By Faith" in our new book, **"What's In Your Toolbox? Building A Strong Spiritual Foundation In Jesus Christ"**.

Learning to walk by faith is important to each one of us because God is not only our creator but also our partner in helping us grow in our Christian faith.

You can be sure God is present with us each day. He wants to bless us abundantly, right where we are, no matter what circumstance we are in at the time.

If we approach each day with expectant faith, we can believe God will touch us and walk with us in a very personal and real way.

I want to share with you my story of learning to walk by faith.

The experience of sharing our faith is one definition of Evangelization. When we tell others how God has touched our life, they are encouraged and helped to deepen their own spiritual life. We can always use each others' help.

As Glenn shares in this book, our family has been through some spiritually challenging times. God has led us through those challenges to a place of calm, loving discipleship with Him. Glenn and I have both become modern-day apostles of Jesus to help others benefit from our experiences, and better understand God and His love for each of us.

Faith and love make all the difference

We have learned the true value of living our lives by walking in the faith of our Lord, Jesus Christ. Faith and love have made all the difference in our lives even as we've faced challenges, disappointments and emotional stress in so many ways.

My own journey of faith is not the result of anything I have done for God but rather what God has done for me. It's about how He has, and how He continues to, rescue and heal me everyday. This is the story of my spiritual walk with Jesus, my story of God's great love for me.

I'll be describing a lot of things that have touched my life, things like how God healed me of the effects of verbal, physical and sexual abuse that happened to me when I was a child.

I'll share about living with an alcoholic parent in a dysfunctional home and how I found out, as an adult, that I had been adopted as a baby.

I'll be sharing about the time that my husband told me that he wanted a divorce. And, I'll share with you what God did to heal our lives and our marriage.

I'll describe some of my trials as a parent and how I made it through so many challenges when one of my children was involved with alcohol and drug abuse.

And, I'll share with you how I handled my mother's death and my feelings of pain, fear, worry, loneliness, rejection, abandonment and my experience of being broken and wounded physically, emotionally and spiritually.

But, most importantly, I'll tell you how God, in His unconditional love and mercy for me, continues to restore and heal me every day.

We all live out the paschal mysteries - those birth, suffering, dying and resurrection moments. However, so many of us just want those resurrection moments. We don't want the suffering and the dying moments.

But, that's just not the way life is.

All people live the paschal mystery, but as Christians, we see that Jesus, through His example, shows us the way to walk through the suffering and the dying moments of life. He has shown us the way, and given us the ability to walk with a peace that is beyond all understanding.

That sounds absurd to the world. But God wants His children to go through life with a joy, a peace and a freedom that is beyond all understanding. He has shown us the way to walk by faith and not by sight.

My story of faith began when I was a very young girl, about the age of four or five. I was sexually abused by a neighbor for some time. After the police came and took a report we never talked about it again in my family.

I remember a girl on the school playground telling me that I made a man go to jail because I was bad and nasty. I remember feelings of guilt and shame that I carried with me for many years.

Several years ago, in prayer, the Lord brought the memory of all of this to my mind and He showed me that I needed to forgive that neighbor. I needed to be healed of all of my shame, guilt, anger and pain. God showed me that it was a burden that I had been carrying around for years and He wanted to set me free.

I know that there are people reading this book who have been sexually abused. Some of you have been healed. Praise God! Some of you are still carrying around the burden of what happened to you. Some of you still carry that pain, guilt, shame and anger. You have not released it yet, and allowed God to heal you.

With God's help, I invite you to let it go, too.

God reminded me that when Jesus went to the cross, and died for us, He did that for all sins, everyone's sins. When Jesus died, He paid the price with His life for the sin that was done against me and for the sin that was done against you. Jesus paid the price in full with His life.

God also reminded me that I was still the one in bondage because I had never forgiven this man.

God was asking me to forgive him so that I could walk in freedom and peace and be free from all of those chains of the past that were holding me in bondage.

Forgiveness Does Not Excuse or Condone The Offense

Forgiveness does not excuse or condone the offense. Forgiveness is to act and do God's will in our life. So, I prayed to God for strength and I forgave this man. Then I asked God to heal me and I asked God to heal him. I made a conscious and deliberate decision to forgive, despite how I felt.

As I prayed, I felt God's loving, healing power. I felt like a little child again, and I visualized myself climbing up into a loving father's lap. He held me and He comforted me. I know God the Father now as Abba, as my Daddy. As I was allowing myself to be loved by Abba, I knew then that God loved this man just as much as He loved me, that His love and His mercy were for both of us.

With God's grace, and my decision to yield my will and my memories of this event to the will of God, He healed me of that pain, anger and shame which I had unconsciously held on to for so many years. This takes time but forgiveness is a decision that needs to be made.

For those reading this who still feel that pain of unforgiveness in your lives, I invite you today to ask God to come into your hearts to heal and restore you like He did for me.

God is just waiting for your decision and your willingness to let go. Sometimes it takes time for the feelings of pain and hurt to pass and this is not a one-time action.

When I was growing up, my father was in the Navy, so we moved around a lot. By the time I was 18 years old we had lived in 20 different cities. I had a hard time feeling like I really belonged anywhere. And it was always difficult trying to make new friends.

My parents only went to church on Easter and Christmas, if that. But, if someone invited my sisters and me to go to church we went along. They were all different churches and different denominations.

In the sixth grade, I fell in love with Jesus. We had learned the story of the Good Shepherd and I memorized the 23rd psalm, which really touched my heart.

In your Bible, turn to Luke 15:4-7. Jesus says, "Who among you, if he owns 100 sheep, and loses one of them, does not leave the 99 and search for the lost one until he finds it? And, when he finds it, he puts it on his shoulders in jubilation and once he arrives home he invites his friends and his neighbors and says to them, Rejoice with me, because I have found my lost sheep. I tell you there will likewise be more joy in heaven over one repentant sinner than over 99 righteous people who have no need to repent."

I remember being so amazed that Jesus, as the Good Shepherd, would leave that flock of 99 and go after that one lost sheep. Because even at that young age I already felt like I was lost and alone - a lost sheep.

Are there times in your life when you feel lost and alone?

I think one of the reasons I felt so alone and scared was the fact that my father was an alcoholic.

It was very hard growing up in a dysfunctional home. Some of you reading this know what I'm talking about.

I knew my father loved us very much. And, I knew he could be very loving and wonderful. I had some great memories of our family when I was a child.

But, as his drinking got worse, so did his verbal abuse.

Because of his personality, and his Navy background, he liked to run a tight ship, even at home. He could be a very hard man at times.

My mother, on the other hand, was loving, gentle, friendly and kind. But, she had no rules at all.

When my dad was out to sea for 9 to 13 months at a time, we lived our lives without conflict and my mother was very lenient. But when my dad came home, everything would change. My sisters and I grew up with such verbal abuse that many times Dad's words would bring us all to tears, even my mother.

I especially hated dinner time on my dad's day off because he'd be drinking all day long. It seemed to be the perfect time for him to start picking on all of us for the things that we didn't do right. Because I was the oldest, it seemed I was most often the one who was in trouble.

I never knew when I'd be sent to my room from the dinner table because I hadn't eaten my dinner the way that he wanted. He put food on our plate at 3, 6 and 9 o'clock and I had to make sure I ate my food clockwise or it would set him off into a rage.

Because of things like that, I grew up with very little confidence. I had low self-esteem.

Still, as a child, I loved my dad, and I loved him as an adult, until the day he died. And, he knew it. When I was a child I'd go fishing with him and I tried to be a tomboy because he said he always wanted a son.

My dad's drinking and abuse got worse as I got older. Later, while I was in college, my dad got physically abusive with me.

My parents separated and later they got a divorce. Even then, I would try so hard to please my dad but I always fell short. I think I felt the same way about God. I wanted to be good and I wanted to please God but I knew so often that I fell short. I thought if only I just tried a little harder, then He'd love me.

Do You Feel Like
You Fall Short With God?

Do you sometimes feel like you fall short with God? Do you feel that if only you could just try a little harder then God would love you, too?

Is your idea of God sometimes like that parent who constantly reminds you of how bad you are and how much you have failed?

Do you see God as someone who keeps score and so you feel you can never do enough good to outweigh all the bad that you do? I think many people have low self-esteem and low self-worth anyway. And I believe there are people reading this book who have grown up with verbal and physical abuse, far worse than I can imagine.

I also believe that some of you have been abused for so long that you don't believe you have or are anything of value.

But, you know what?

That's just not true.

God says, in Isaiah 43:4, that "you are precious in my eyes and glorious because I love you."

That is such an awesome thought. Even after all these years, I know I haven't grasped the reality of that truth completely. Just think, God said that we, His children, are precious to Him and He loves us. I believe that if we could really absorb what that means none of us would ever have a low self-esteem problem again.

We would all face this world everyday in confidence. We would say to others, "Do to me whatever you want. It doesn't matter to me what you think, because I am precious and glorious to my God, and He loves me."

Have you ever felt - or been made to feel - you aren't precious and loved? Do you know this is a lie that Satan tries to tell us all the time? It's a lie because God says you are precious and glorious in His sight. You are loved by your Creator, your God.

Who are you going to believe, Satan or God?

You don't have to do a thing to earn God's love. He just loves you. He created you just the way you are and He knows everything about you, and me, and it doesn't matter.

God just loves you.

God can heal anything. That includes any pain, any situations or anything you have to deal with. God wants us to invite Him into the broken, wounded areas of our lives and accept His healing love and mercy.

But, He will require us to extend love and forgiveness to our enemies, those who have hurt us.

Now, I have forgiven my father, for his sickness and for his sins against me, and I love my dad very much.

Look at your own life. Who is your enemy? Who has hurt you the most?

God is asking you to extend forgiveness to those who have hurt you so you can be healed and free.

When I Met My Future Husband

I'd like to share with you now a little bit about my young adult years and my married life.

I met my husband Glenn in college. He was a Catholic who loved God and his church very much. And I wanted what he had, so I became Catholic. We were married in the church in April of 1970.

Right after our oldest daughter, Christina, was born I found out, in a very painful way, that I had been adopted as a baby. I had no idea that I had been adopted and it came as quite a shock to me. I felt so much pain. I felt rejected, unwanted and wounded by my birth mother giving me up for adoption.

Because I was adopted, I wondered if that was why I always felt a lack of belonging in my family, even though I was much loved by my parents. But, God helped me to recall the passage from the Bible in Isaiah 49:14-15, when God said, "Even should a mother forget her child, I will never forget you."

Now, some of you reading about this experience may be adopted, too. And, you may feel rejected by your mother or feel abandoned or go through times when you feel like you just don't belong. Realize that all of us, at one time or another, feel unwanted and rejected, for many reasons.

But, God reminded me, and He reminds you, that there are no orphans in God's family. We all belong to Him. We are all adopted and heirs to God Himself.

God showed me that instead of feeling rejection, I needed to pray for my biological parents and let go of the feelings that I had of being an unwanted child.

I especially prayed for my mother and I asked God to relieve her of any guilt and pain that she might have had, or maybe she still has today - to give her His peace.

In prayer, God asked me to think of her and what pain she must have gone through as a young, unwed mother, and the scandal she must have suffered in making that kind of decision.

In Colossians 3:15 the Bible says, "Christ's peace must reign in your heart since, as members of the one body, we have been called to that peace. Dedicate yourself to thankfulness."

I started doing just that. I prayed and I thanked my mother for making that difficult choice to have me and to give me away for adoption, rather than having an abortion.

God flooded my heart with mercy and compassion for my biological parents and He gave me a new appreciation for my adoptive parents.

If we will dedicate ourselves to thankfulness, it will become very difficult to feel badly about our own situation. We need to keep an attitude of gratitude and then we will more readily see how God is working in our lives and how much He does love us.

After Glenn and I had been married for several years, we started a disillusionment phase in our relationship.

We had two small children who were only 13 months apart. We had really bad money problems, and we got all caught up in our jobs, kids and just all the things that were going on. We stopped going to church and we stopped caring for one another. We had no life together and no love for one another.

There was a "Grand Canyon" between us

I remember laying in bed together for several nights and thinking how amazing it is that two people could be in the same bed, only inches apart, but feel like the Grand Canyon was between us. Have you ever felt that way in your marriage? Did you ever feel like your marriage was slowly dying and yet you felt there was nothing you could do about it?

Through God's love and mercy we did have a resurrection moment in our marriage. My best friend encouraged us to make a Marriage Encounter weekend, where God showed us that we have a Sacrament and that marriage was our vocation in life.

At that moment we fell in love with each other, with our God and with our church all over again. Actually, love is a decision, not a feeling.

We went back to our church and it seemed we just couldn't do enough. We were a team couple for Marriage Encounter, we were working in youth ministry; we were members of the choir and involved in anything else that needed to be done. We attended a Life in the Spirit seminar and God turned up the flame of desire for us to serve.

We were so happy as a family.

Glenn and I attended a week-long school of evangelization and we got even more excited about working for the Lord.

We heard so many wonderful things, such as learning that we were called to be apostles and that we had a job to do today in the church, just like Peter and Paul did back in the time of Jesus.

After that school, Glenn quit his job. We decided that we both wanted to serve the Lord full time.

And then, through unbelievable acts of God that we call Godcidentals, not coincidentals, Glenn became the director of youth ministry for the Diocese of Boise, Idaho. I became a pastoral associate for our parish and a leader for a women's prayer group.

Life was just great!

...for a couple of years.

But, as time passed, we got all caught up in doing our own thing again.

Glenn's territory was the entire state of Idaho, all 86,000 square miles. So he was always gone again, especially nights and weekends.

We started growing apart - again.

That was also a time when I started to realize that it was quite possible to do Godly work without God being at the center of all of it. You can fool yourself and others for a short amount of time, but the truth will come forth.

Our schedules were so full that we were left with no time to spend with each other.

Then, one day, out of the blue, Glenn told me that he wanted a divorce and that he didn't love me anymore. I had feelings of shock, disbelief, doubt, fear, rejection, loneliness, pain and complete abandonment. I felt like a hole had just been ripped out from the center of me and my entire life was caving in around me.

I questioned how God could have let that happen.

Some of you, I'm sure, know exactly what I'm talking about. Others may not know those feelings that come from a word like "divorce." But certainly other devastating things may have occurred in your life that - like the reality of the word divorce -

made you question God, asking Him, "God, how could you let something like this happen to me or to my family?"

You, like me, at some point in your life, may have experienced more pain than you ever could have imagined and wondered how you could handle that situation.

I'd like to share how God helped me through this time of devastation. My hope is that my experiences of the power of God in the midst of this devastation might be of use to you now or that you might keep it in your heart and use it for a later time in your life.

Remember, we all live the paschal mystery: birth, suffering, dying and resurrection. God gave me some powerful scriptures and insight into how to apply them.

He also sent me a few strong prayer warriors to help me in this battle. Yes, it was a battle, because I knew this was a war. My enemy, however, was Satan and his evil spirit of divorce. I knew it wasn't Glenn.

God showed me that I had to stand and face the enemy of divorce, not only for me but for my two girls and for my grandchildren. You see, I came from a long line of divorces in my family. My own mother and father, as well as each of their mothers and fathers had gotten divorces or separations.

I knew this chain of divorce just had to be broken in my family line.

You Shall Call
And The Lord Will Answer

The first scripture God gave me was Isaiah 58:9, "You shall call and the Lord will answer. You shall cry for help and He will say, 'Here I am.'"

I did call for help and God assured me He was with me and that I wasn't alone in this battle. He was there.

So whatever battle you're going through, please know that you are not in it alone. God is with you. You can depend on the

Lord. I felt God's assurance that Glenn and I had a Sacramental union and that we would get through this and be healed.

Now I didn't know how God could make this happen, because at that time I didn't even like Glenn any more, much less love him. I kept asking God, "What is your will in this matter?" And then I knew, beyond a shadow of a doubt, that it was God's will for us to stay together. We were a Sacrament!

I told God I didn't know how He would work it out but that I would do my part to remain faithful to our marriage.

Are there areas in your life that you are wondering how God will help you work it out? It looks impossible in the natural world! That's why God tells us to walk by faith and not by sight.

We are called to do our part in the battle, which means praying and not giving up, for the battle belongs to the Lord. We aren't suppose to believe what we see in the natural world. We are supposed to believe what God says.

God led me to the most wonderful scripture and insight into its meaning, and I'd like to share it with you. You can apply it right now to so many situations in your life, and always hold on to it for later occasions. God urged me to read St. Paul's letter to the Philippians, 4:4-9.

"Rejoice in the Lord, always, I say again, rejoice. Everyone should see how unselfish you are. The Lord is near. Dismiss all anxiety from your mind. Present your needs to God in all forms of prayer and petition, full of gratitude. Then, God's peace, which is beyond all understanding, will stand guard over your heart and mind in Christ Jesus."

Direct Your Thoughts
To All That Is True and Virtuous

Finally, St. Paul writes, "Your thoughts should be wholly directed to all that is true, all that deserves respect, all that is honest, pure, admirable, decent, virtuous, and worthy of praise. Live according to what you have learned and accepted, what you have heard me say and seen me do. Then will the God of Peace be with you."

After reading that passage, I asked God if He was sure about leading me to this scripture. As I continued to pray, He led me to understand and believe that Bible passage in my heart and to see how it applied to my situation.

Can you believe this for you and your situation?

Now the first thing it says to do is rejoice. It's so important that God says it again, "I say again, rejoice!"

That's a pretty tough order when all you feel like doing is crying and getting angry. But, one of the first things I realized was that I would not get through this operating on a "feeling" level. I had to follow God's direction.

So that was my first lesson, not to act or react on my feelings, which changed moment by moment. But to make a conscious and deliberate decision to be obedient to the will of God.

Now some of God's scripture direction was, for a long time, puzzling to me, particularly the passage that said, "Everyone should see how unselfish you are."

Part of that scripture may puzzle you, as it puzzled me. I was months into this journey before I really understood the meaning of, "Everyone should see how unselfish you are."

I prayed this scripture passage daily, sometimes ten times a day, to get through those emotionally hard times.

What I came to understand is that when you don't act according to your feelings, but instead make your decisions in obedience to God's will despite your feelings, this is a very unselfish act.

I learned the truth of what Jesus means in scripture when He says, "God is with you. Know that you are not in this battle alone. He is right by your side." The next line says, "Dismiss all anxiety from your mind."

What jumped out at me was the word, "all."

He didn't say you could hold onto some of your anxiety. Jesus said "all anxiety." It was not just a suggestion, it was more like a command, to not allow any anxiety into your mind.

That was very difficult for me because my mother was a worrier, so I saw that constantly as I was growing up. She seemed to feel that she wasn't doing a good job as a mother unless she was worrying.

And that example influenced my own life.

Great News For Worriers!
Become A Great Warrior – For God!

Well, I have some great news for you if you are a good worrier. Instead, you can be a great warrior for the Lord.

Worriers have their focus on how big their problem is. What you really need to focus on is how big your God is. God is looking for warriors to do battle for His kingdom - not worriers!

Next, Jesus said, "Present your needs to God in every form of prayer and in petitions full of gratitude."

I asked God how in the world can I do that?

Well, God showed me that to present your needs to Him full of gratitude means to see the situation as already resolved, in God's way, a way that would give Him the glory. And I knew that it would give God glory to heal and restore our sacrament of marriage.

So, as I continued praying all those months, I began believing that God would do it. I began to see with eyes of faith and not with eyes of sight.

That was certainly not following my feelings, because everything around me looked absolutely hopeless. It looked like our marriage was already dead.

The next line of scripture says, "God's own peace, which is beyond all understanding, will stand guard over your heart and your mind in Christ Jesus."

Then, God showed me what I like to refer to as my "glory bubble."

Every time Glenn and I would get together, a lot of painful and hurtful things were being said.

So what I did was to visualize myself inside this protective bubble. covered and protected by God from head to toe, inside my "glory bubble."

I knew that if words were said to hurt me that I would let them come into my heart and my mind and that later on I would have to work at releasing that pain and releasing those feelings of unforgiveness.

So each time we met and hurtful things were said, I just placed myself inside this glory bubble, imagining it covered me from the top of my head to the tips of my toes. It was truly a bubble of protection. The words would just hit it and slide right off. That way, I never took them into my heart.

This was a great help to me. I know, of course, that it must have infuriated Satan, because he wanted me to develop a hard heart and live with a lot of angry thoughts.

Instead, I was letting God's peace guard my heart and my mind.

Now, I am not telling you that this was easy. I still felt the pain but those hurtful words stirred up inside of me such a Godly righteousness, which allowed me to stand and face this enemy called divorce and strengthened me in the battle.

The next line of that scripture says "your thoughts should be wholly" - not partially, mind you - but "wholly directed to all that is true, all that deserves respect, all that is honest, pure, admirable, decent, virtuous and worthy of praise."

You know, that just doesn't leave much room for stinking thinking. There's only room for those victorious thoughts, not those "what if" thoughts, which is the Devil's way of making us wallow in worry, doubt and fear.

Fear, I think, is the really big one to avoid because, you know, battles like this are waged in our minds, so what we think about really matters. Our thoughts will either help us or hurt us.

In Romans 12:2 Christ tells us that we must renew our minds and put on the mind of Christ. Then scripture says, in Philippians 4:9, "Live according to what you have learned and accepted, what you have heard me say and seen me do."

I've learned and accepted that God is more powerful than Satan.

You know what?

We can win these spiritual battles. We will win. Victory will be ours, with God's help.

Jesus meant for me to believe and live my life as though my marriage was already healed.

Either God is God or He is not. The promises of His word are either true or they are not. The last line of that scripture says, "Then will the God of peace be with you." God promises us peace. And peace is what we need so badly when we're in the middle of a battle.

God's peace helped me get through every single day of pain.

Have you gone through, or are you currently going through, a devastating battle that is like a crucifixion in your life?

When you pray to God for help, remember that nothing, absolutely nothing, is too great for God to handle. And, remember, too, that God wants to help us. We are His children. He created us.

Someone once wrote, "God never tires of helping us. We are the ones who tire of asking for God's help."

Apply these messages of Philippians 4:4-9 to whatever you're going through, and let God's peace be with you. The experiences Glenn and I lived through, with God's help, prove that God and His scriptures can help you, too.

After all of our trials and tribulations, 13 months to the day after Glenn asked for a divorce, God showed us His mercy and compassion by restoring our broken marriage.

We look at that as truly a resurrection moment in our marriage.

Finally, after all of the months of heartache, pain and battle, Glenn and I renewed our marriage vows before hundreds of friends and family. Glenn stood at the pulpit that day and asked for my forgiveness and the forgiveness of our daughters, our community and our God.

Again, God in His mercy was creating something new between us. He wasn't just fixing up our old marriage, He was making our marriage new and better than ever before.

I learned so much from this experience.

I learned that I could love more than I ever imagined I could, because Jesus taught me to love, not with my own love, but with His love.

Our own love comes to an end. But the love of Jesus never ends, never runs out. As children of God we are allowed the privilege of tapping into and using the love of Jesus, through the Holy Spirit.

When we live our lives by the guidance of the Holy Spirit, we tap into the love of Jesus. We are able to love with that unconditional and limitless love of God, our Father, not with just our own love, which is very conditional and has its limits.

But, unfortunately, Glenn sought forgiveness from everyone except himself.

You know, sometimes we are the hardest person to forgive.

Have you found that true in your life? I have certainly found it true in mine.

Glenn Returns
To The Corporate World

At this point, although our marriage was saved and blessed, Glenn felt so unworthy to serve God and His church that we left ministry work. We moved back to San Diego and Glenn went back to the corporate world.

During the next couple of years, our youngest daughter began having a lot of trouble in school. Then she got involved with the wrong group of friends. She became angry and rebellious and soon was out of control.

We just tried everything to reach her. We tried loving her more, finding counseling, applying more discipline but nothing seemed to work. She was obviously on a downhill spiral. It was really getting worse and worse. She started running away from home, and even tried to commit suicide.

Of course, we felt so helpless. Have you ever felt totally helpless when it came to your children and their lives? You look at them and their actions and you're just at a loss about what to do?

Well, next came one of the hardest decisions we ever had to make. We admitted her into a rehab hospital - and left her there. She hated us for doing that and she wasn't willing to cooperate for a long time.

All Glenn and I could do was pray.

Fortunately, our faith community was there for us. We had a lot of friends supporting us and we experienced their prayers holding us together.

Have you ever experienced being connected to community and feeling their love and the support of their prayers holding you together? That's why we all need to be connected.

You see, God never intended for us to walk this earthly walk alone. We are on this journey together because we are the Church. Slowly, over time, through the grace of God, she started her healing process.

Today, she is a strong and wonderful person. She is now married and has a beautiful daughter, and I know that she knows and loves God. I'm standing in the gap for her by praying every single day.

Is there a child or grandchild you are standing in the gap for today?

Please pray Isaiah 43:5-6, which says, "Fear not, for I am with you. From the East I will bring back your descendants and from the West I will gather you. I will say to the North, give them up, and to the South, hold not back. Bring back my sons from afar and my daughters from the ends of the Earth."

You know God has them covered, from the north, east, west and south, even from the ends of the Earth. God will bring back our children and our grandchildren. That is His promise. That's not my promise.

Prayer Is The Most Important Thing We Can Do!

Do you know that prayer is the most important thing that we can do?

That's our part in the battle. Walk by faith, not by sight. We should never underestimate the power of persistent prayer.

We can move past all that pain and enter into the throne room of grace and lay our petitions before God, full of gratitude.

Our prayers need to be bold and full of hope. We need to ask Jesus to help us increase our faith and believe that He can and will heal and restore. But, we don't need to know how He's going to do it.

For me, if I knew God's plan, I'd probably try to step in, take over and botch it all up.

We need to make an act of faith, to choose to believe and then act as though God has already done it. Even though we might not be able to see how, we must be able to see the situation with eyes of faith.

Remember that Hebrews 11:1-2 says, "Faith is confident assurance concerning what we hope for and conviction about things we do not see."

What are you hoping for today? What do you not see that you need to believe? Believe that God is working to resolve your problem in a way that will give Him glory. God wants us to have, and live with, His Joy, according to John 15:11.

Also, Hebrews 11:6 says, "Without faith it is impossible to please God." Do you want to please God? I know that I do. So operate in faith.

Does The Thought Of Death Make You Fearful?

Now there is just one other topic that I would like to touch on.

That topic is death.

I used to be so fearful of death that I could hardly talk about it without crying.

In September 1992, my mother died suddenly, at the age of 66. It was a real shock to me. We were very close. I think sometimes you just don't know how much you really love someone until they're gone.

I guess I thought that we had many, many more years to share our lives and our love together. But you know, we just never know when it's our time, or the time for a loved one, to go home to be with the Lord.

So, we need to make every day count and not take each other for granted. We need to enjoy and treasure those special, wonderful people that God has placed in our lives.

We need to remember to make every single day count. We must live in the present moment. Yesterday is gone, and no matter how hard we try, we cannot enter into tomorrow. God is eternal. God always has been, is now and always will be. We can only live in the present moment so "now" is the only time we have.

If we want to love, the only time that we have to love is now. If we want to trust, hope, forgive, have joy and peace, the only time we can do it is now.

If you want to pray and stand in the gap for someone, or if you want to serve God with all your heart, the only time you can do it is now.

My faith and my belief is that my mother is in heaven, face to face with God. That thought gives me much joy and hope and has taken my fear away. So love today all of those special people that God has placed in your life.

Our marriage was healed and our family restored. Glenn was back in the fast lane of the corporate world. However, I sensed that my husband was wrestling with God. There was a hole inside of him that money, power, recognition and authority would not fill.

No matter what title the world had given him, Glenn still knew that his true identity was as an apostle of the Lord Jesus Christ.

There was a still, small voice within him that kept saying, "I want you." Glenn knew it was the voice of the Holy Spirit, but he felt he was unworthy to serve the Lord and His church because of his past failures.

Over time, God reminded Glenn of how St. Peter had denied Christ three times, how St. Thomas had doubted that Jesus had truly risen from the dead. In spite of those failures, our Lord called these men to proclaim the Gospel to the ends of the world.

After many years of healing, prayer, discernment, dialogue and guidance by the Holy Spirit, we decided to be obedient to the Lord's call. We turned our backs on the "Gospel of the World" and made the choice to live for the "Gospel of Christ."

It has been an amazing journey so far. Jesus keeps saying "follow me" and we keep saying "Yes, Lord." Together, we serve an amazing, awesome and mighty God!

Glenn and I have now been in full-time ministry since July 1992. And, like every other aspect of our lives, our walk in this ministry has reflected Christ's pascal mystery - the birth, suffering, dying and wonderful resurrection moments.

We travel the country doing missions, retreats and days of renewal. We are living witnesses to the sacrament of marriage, showing others how God can and will use all things for good for those who love the Lord.

You know, we all try and fail so many times to live our lives by giving God the glory, but all God asks of us is to try. He asks for our willingness to walk by faith rather than by sight.

What I'm learning every day is that I need to grow in faith and surrender everything to the Lord. My safety, my security, my finances and my family. I have to trust and give them all to the Lord. Without Jesus being at the center of everything, and the guidance of the Holy Spirit, it is all in vain.

You know, God is either God or He's not. His promises are either true for us or they're not. And, the Bible is either the greatest story that's ever been told or it's the greatest lie that's ever been written. It's either one or the other, it cannot be both.

What is it for you today?

For me, it's following the true, living word of God. What I'm developing in my life is a real sense of how desperate this world is for a Savior and how important my role - and your role - is in bringing that message to the world.

You know, we live in a time of evil. Almost everything society professes goes completely against the values and the principles of God.

People are desperate for the mercy, compassion and the message of God. We need to hear and live the good news, that there is a savior for all of us and His name is Jesus, the Good Shepherd who always cares enough to go after His lost sheep.

He's sending us. We are the hands and the feet of Jesus. He's sending us with a message of love and forgiveness, not just with our words but also with our actions.

"Jesus calls us to love our enemies, to do good to those who hate us, to bless those who curse us and to pray for those who mistreat us," Luke 6:27-28.

Read Luke 6:27-28. In the "Our Father," which is the prayer that Jesus wanted us to know, we say "Forgive us our trespasses as we forgive those who trespass against us."

I believe that it's unforgiveness that keeps us in bondage. It steals our joy, our peace and our freedom. God says, "Know the truth and the truth will set us free." What pain or bondage in your life do you need to be set free?

God has shown me in my life, over and over again, that I need to forgive. That's a gift I give to myself as well as to the one who hurt me. God always gives us a choice. He says, in Deuteronomy 30:19, "Choose this day the way of life or death."

God gives us the way. God sent His own son, Jesus, to be our model, to show us that the right way to live is to embrace our own cross and be guided by God's word.

Whether we are a believer or not, we all have crosses in our lives to bear. But Jesus promises us that if we will pick up our cross and carry it to the Father, and lean on Him and His truth, then we will be set free.

Now, this is our choice. To surrender our will to the Father. And, when we do this, God will change our Good Friday into Easter joy. We will experience the resurrection even though that joy is seen as an absurdity to the world.

If we choose not to forgive, we are sentencing ourselves to a lifetime of pain and despair. God doesn't want this for His children. He gave us a way to walk in peace.

God said, "I have come to give you life, and to give it to you abundantly."

But, fear keeps us from that abundant living. F. E. A. R., meaning: False Evidence Appearing Real. I've heard this for many years. This is the lie that Satan tries to tell us and we buy into it all the time.

When I was fearful and I prayed, God showed me a choice, He showed me what faith is – F.A.I.T.H. Father Affirming my Inheritance of Truth and Hope.

Faith, like grace, is a gift from God.

A measure of faith is given to each one of us. We can either bury it and forget about it, and drift farther from our Creator, or we can use it and see our faith develop and grow, with God's help. As children of God we are called to exercise our faith so that it grows, takes over and fills us so doubt and fear and worry and anxiety will have no room in our lives.

Over and over again, in scripture, God tells us, His children, do not be afraid. I've discovered that fear isn't a lack of believing.

Fear is believing in the wrong thing.

It's believing in the natural realm, in what we see with our sight. It's listening and believing what Satan wants to tell us.

But faith, on the other hand, is believing what God says and shows us.

Remember, F.A.I.T.H. means our Father Affirming our Inheritance of Truth and Hope.

It is our inheritance because we are "born again" children of God, and we are His heirs to the kingdom. It is the truth that sets us free.

It is our hope that gives us the ability to walk in the suffering, dying moments of our life knowing, deep in our hearts, that God is in charge and He will turn all of our sorrows into resurrection moments.

He is who He says He is.

God's promises are true, for you and for me.

Remember, God has told us that you are precious and glorious in His eyes and He loves you.

I love you, too.

May God bless you always.

Our Closing Prayer

Heavenly Father, you know my heart. You are aware of the joy, hurt and pain that it holds. I want to walk and grow in my faith. Help me to surrender any concern, worry, anxiety or fear that I may have deep within me.

I want to be a mighty warrior for you and not a worrier. I can only do this with your grace. Help me to forgive myself or anyone who has hurt me. Grant me the abundant life that you want and have promised for me.

Lord, I ask and I receive at this moment your peace, hope, love and joy. I ask all these desires of my heart in and through the precious and holy name of my Lord and Savior, Jesus Christ.

Amen.

Call To Action

1) In what areas of my life do I desire and need more faith?

2) What are the steps I can take to grow in faith in this area?

3) Do I need to give the gift of forgiveness to myself or to anyone else in my life? If the answer is "Yes," am I willing to ask for God's grace to act?

4) What are the specific steps I can make to move myself from the "chains" of unforgiveness to the freedom of forgiveness?

Chapter 4

Unforgiveness – A Terminal Illness

From the time we are born until we leave this Earth, our lives are a series of choices. We have all made many good choices, and we have all made choices that we wish we hadn't made.

However, once in a while, we make a choice that will follow us through eternity. Those are the choices we really need to think and pray about before acting.

St. John Paul II often spoke about our spiritual journey on this Earth. He said it has three primary steps. The first step starts in our hearts, the second extends to the believing community and the third step will eventually reach out to all of humanity.

In this chapter you will be going on a spiritual journey that hopefully will take you, if necessary, from unforgiveness to forgiveness to reconciliation. Reconciliation means re-establishing and re-connecting broken relationships. When Jesus Christ went to the cross over 2,000 years ago, He re-established and re-connected the broken, damaged relationship between God and all of humanity.

If Jesus was to shine the light of His Gospel on any and all of the relationships in your life, past or present, would any of those relationships be in need of forgiveness and reconciliation? In other words, are you currently holding any anger, resentment, bitterness or unforgiveness against anyone? You might as well be honest with yourself because God knows the answer to that question.

I used to have one of the hardest hearts of anyone you would ever meet. I wore unforgiveness like a badge of honor. I was very good at what I call "cut and run." If you hurt me in any way, I simply wrote you off. As far as I was concerned, you no longer existed. Maybe you know someone like that. Maybe <u>you</u> are someone like that.

"FORGIVE THEM"

Jesus Christ showed us the importance of forgiveness when
He forgave those who crucified Him, setting an example for us to
follow in our own lives.

Because I didn't understand this biblical and spiritual topic of forgiveness, and wouldn't do anything about it, I was filled with anger, bitterness and pain.

I found it easier to hold on to revenge rather than work through the process of forgiveness and healing. When the pain became so intense, I started to learn and study about unforgiveness and forgiveness. When I made the choice to act on what I had learned, I experienced a peace and healing I never thought was possible.

I have learned through my own life and by ministering to so many people over the years, that if we don't address this head on, unforgiveness will become a terminal illness. It will kill us physically, emotionally and spiritually.

I have now reached a point in my life where I want forgiveness from my Heavenly Father. If there is anything I have done or am currently doing that is blocking that forgiveness, I want to know what it is and I am going to resolve it.

I continually ask my Lord, "Is there anybody in my life that I need to forgive? Is there anyone that I am holding anger, bitterness or resentment against?" When He tells me, and usually I already know, I do whatever I can to forgive that person.

Is it easy? NO!

Forgiveness is not a normal human response to being hurt. But I want my Heavenly Father's forgiveness, so I do what Jesus says to do, by listening to Jesus who speaks to us everyday.

I have mentioned all of the above because this is a topic that most people don't want to think about or talk about. And because we often work so hard to avoid this basic and necessary spiritual principle, we don't do anything to resolve it.

This chapter will give you the opportunity to not only to look into your heart and mind, but to do something about it. So, if at this point, you haven't thrown this book across the room, stomped on it and set it on fire, let's continue.

Over the past two plus decades, Linda and I have had the opportunity to preach and teach on this subject of unforgiveness and forgiveness. I feel confident in saying that at least 95 percent of the people who listened would say that unforgiveness is not a good or healthy thing, and that it certainly goes against the teaching of Jesus Christ.

So, why do we still choose to do it? One of the key reasons is our society has become so riddled and permeated with bitterness, resentment, revenge and unforgiveness that if we're not careful we can almost consider it a normal response to life. It is destroying marriages, tearing families apart and dividing church communities.

Sin is often referred to as missing the mark, God's mark. Because we are all sinful people and therefore struggle with forgiveness throughout our lives, we all miss the mark on this issue.

Hundreds of books have been written on this topic of forgiveness. It is not an easy Biblical and spiritual principle to grasp and implement in our lives. I found an anonymous quote which says, "Nobody is perfect, no one has it easy and everybody has issues. You never know what people are going through. So pause before you start judging, criticizing or holding on to past hurts. Everybody is fighting their own unique battles."

I am a husband, father, grandfather and deacon, but I consider myself an ordinary man who has fought many personal battles and quite often struggle with my own spirituality. However, because I have found it helpful to be practical in my approach to God and His Word, I have narrowed the forgiveness process to three steps. At times, a person can work through these three steps rather quickly and move on. However, in other situations, it can take months or years.

- The first step is **intellectual**. It becomes a choice and a decision of the will to let go of the desire to get even with someone who has hurt you.
- The second step is **emotional**. To be completely healed and set free, we must be willing to work through the feelings, hurt and pain of past or current offenses against us. As long as we make the choice to hold on, deny or bury

the pain of the past, we will remain captives and prisoners of past offenses. **We cannot heal what we do not feel!**

- The third and final step is **spiritual.** We reach the point where letting go, surrendering and giving it to God is more important than holding on to the past.

To further illustrate this three-step process, let's look at a scripture passage that appears in only one of the Canonical Gospels in the New Testament. It will further break open and illustrate the three-step process I just outlined. I believe that God will reveal some new, powerful and possibly life changing awareness in this parable.

I encourage you not to allow your familiarity of this scripture to steal the freshness of what the Holy Spirit wants to place in your mind and heart.

Before going any further, please read the Gospel of Luke 15:11-32.

A Parable Of
Unforgiveness And Forgiveness

Jesus said to them, "A man has two sons. The younger of them said to his father, give me the share of the estate that is coming to me. So the father divided up the property."

Let's stop and analyze this situation. Back in the days when this parable was preached by Jesus, the Jewish law was similar to our inheritance laws today. No heir, son or daughter, was to get anything until the father had died. So there must have been a major problem between the father and his younger son. When the son asked his father for his share of the inheritance while his father was still alive, he was in essence saying to his father, "As far as I'm concerned, you are dead."

Can you imagine how this must have broken the heart of his father? It also brought shame and humiliation to the father and the rest of his family when word of this reached the other members of the community. Can you see how anger, bitterness, revenge and unforgiveness can numb the senses and blind us to the truth?

Another powerful point of this scripture is that the father loved his son so much that in spite of the hurt, pain, humiliation and shame he must have been feeling, he still gave him his share of the inheritance. What an awesome father!

Jesus continues, "Some days later this younger son collected all his belongings and went off to a distant land, where he squandered his money on a life of debauchery and decadence. When he had freely spent everything, a severe famine broke out in that country and he found himself in dire need. So, he was hired by one of the local citizens who sent him to his farm to tend the swine. He was so hungry that he longed to eat his fill of the food scraps that the pigs ate, but nobody gave him any."

Perhaps in just a few days or maybe weeks, this young man had lost everything that his father had worked for all of his life. Think of the greed, pride and selfishness of this son. It reminds me that the root cause of any sin is selfishness. In other words, "I want what I want right now, and I don't care what God or anyone else thinks or says." When we choose to sin, we put our desire and will above the will of God. We either learn and repent from those choices, or we carry them throughout all eternity.

This young man finds himself without any money or possessions and he reaches the point where he is willing to eat the leftover food that the pigs wouldn't eat. This man was desperate! He had everything he ever needed back home with his father. He had money, possessions, a great family and the love of his father. Who could ask or want for anything more than that?

The next scripture verse changes this young man's life forever. "Coming to his senses at last, he said, "How many of father's hired workers have more than enough to eat but here I am, dying from hunger." He was separated from his father and family and he was broke, hungry and dirty. He realized that where he was, physically, emotionally and spiritually – was not where he wanted to be any longer. Have you ever been in that situation? I have and it's like being in an earthly hell.

The son had finally reached the first step of the process of forgiveness. He came to the point intellectually that he no longer wanted to seek revenge or get even with his father. However, he could have stayed there the rest of his life, repeatedly coming to his senses, without taking the next step to healing and a new beginning.

Have you ever heard the definition of insanity? "Doing the same thing in the same way over and over and expecting a different result is insanity!"

As Linda and I travel North America giving our missions and retreats, we encounter many people who have come to their senses. They have gained an awareness and understanding that they have sinned. They are finally willing to repent, change their ways and embrace and follow Jesus Christ.

Jesus continues His parable, "I will get up and return to my father and say to him, 'Father, I have sinned against God and against you. I no longer deserve to be called your son. Treat me like one of your hired workers.' With that he sets off for his father's house."

What a moment of repentance, humility and conversion! The son verbalizes what he believes will be his penance. At this point, this young man begins the second step of the forgiveness process, which is emotional. He begins to get in touch with the hurt, pain and all the feelings of his actions, feeling the shame, guilt, humiliation, fear, doubt and the struggle to forgive himself.

Remember, we cannot heal what we do not feel.

On his journey home, I imagine he might be thinking, "My father is going to rip me up. He is going to make me jump through hoops and pay back every penny I wasted and lost." He was preparing for revenge and payback.

This parable continues, "While he was still a long way off, his father caught sight of him and was moved with compassion. He ran out to meet him, threw his arms around his neck and kissed him."

To the son's surprise, his father does not display anger, bitterness or revenge, but only unconditional love, forgiveness and mercy. He says, "Father, I have sinned against God and against you, I no longer deserve to be called your son."

But, it's as if his father doesn't even hear what his son is saying. The father is so happy, thrilled and grateful to have his son back, he's not even listening to the penance that his son rehearsed on his long journey home.

The father continues with great joy, "Quick, bring out the finest robe and put it on him, put a ring on his finger and shoes on his feet. Take the fatted calf and kill it. Let us eat and celebrate, because this son of mine was dead and has come back to life. He was lost and is found."

Then, the celebration began.

The son experiences the third step, which is spiritual, when he lets it all go. Don't you wish you could have been there to see all of this unfold? When reconciliation takes place between two people who have had a disconnected relationship, it is celebration time!

The same is true when it comes to us and our heavenly Father. When we sin through some act of selfishness and wander away from God, He watches and eagerly awaits our return home. When I have humbled myself and sought forgiveness and reconciliation with my Heavenly Father, He has always greeted me with open arms of love, forgiveness and mercy. I just melt into His arms with gratitude and humility.

Now, you would think that this parable is over. But, it's not. Up to this point, Jesus has laid out a powerful and moving illustration of forgiveness and reconciliation. Jesus now shows us what can happen if we refuse to forgive.

"Now the older son was out in the field," Jesus says in scripture, "As he neared the house, he heard the sound of music and dancing. He called one of the servants and asked him the reason for the dancing and music. The servant answered, 'Your brother is home, and your father has killed the fatted calf because he has him back in good health.' "

You would think that the older brother would be thrilled with what has happened, but unforgiveness and envy have taken over.

"He became angry and would not go in the house," scripture tells us. "His father came out and began to plead with him. He said to his father in reply, 'For years now I have slaved for you. I never disobeyed one of your orders, yet you never gave me so much as a goat to celebrate with my friends. Then when this son of yours returns after having gone through your money and property with prostitutes, you kill the fatted calf for him.' "

The older son is now trying to remind the father of what had happened, trying to break up this new relationship, even though there's already been forgiveness and reconciliation. He's trying to drive a wedge between the father and his brother. His efforts aren't working. His father reminds him,

"My son, you are with me always, and everything I have is yours. But we must celebrate and rejoice because your brother was dead and has come to life. He was lost and was found."

I have often acted like the older brother and I can tell you, it is a dead end road. The celebration was going on in the Father's house and my anger, bitterness and unforgiveness prevented me from going in.

Again, I ask you, is there any anger, resentment or unforgiveness in your heart towards someone, and is it keeping you from the celebration of forgiveness and reconciliation?

Forgiveness is a journey of faith. But whether it's easy or difficult, at some point we reach a very critical crossroads. We either choose to forgive or we choose to hold on to that unforgiveness. We will ultimately become responsible for the consequences of our choice of unforgiveness.

Clearing Up Some Misunderstandings

I used to have many misunderstandings about this topic of unforgiveness which hindered me from being obedient to my Lord and experiencing the peace and healing I wanted. Let's take a look at a few basic principles about forgiveness.

Forgiveness is a gift from God. With God's grace and our willingness to do what our Lord asks, we can truly be set free of our captivity. Our Lord would never ask us to do something that He would not help us do. The will of God will never take us where the grace of God cannot protect us.

The first and most important person to forgive is our self. We cannot give to someone else what we refuse to give to ourselves.

Not to forgive is a choice to remain a victim of those who have hurt us. Forgiveness means allowing God to help us free ourselves of the anger, resentment, bitterness, revenge and sorrow that can be destructive to us if we continue to carry it. If we refuse to forgive someone, we allow that person to continue to control us and have power over us.

Forgiveness does not mean forgetting. Forgiveness and memory loss have nothing to do with each other. The phrase "forgive and forget" has been a stumbling block for so many people over the years. When we forgive, we don't forget, we just move on.

Forgiveness does not mean approving or validating the actions or behavior of the person(s) who have hurt you. If someone has hurt you in any way, physically, emotionally, verbally, sexually, that will never be OK. But when we forgive, we are finally being good to ourselves.

Forgiveness does not always mean re-establishing a relationship. God does not call us to continually put ourselves in situations that might be verbally, emotionally or physically damaging. Some relationships are simply not safe.

Forgiveness cannot be proven by our feelings. It takes courage and grace to look at a person in the eyes and forgive them or ask them to forgive us. At times, it makes more sense to call, email, text, write a note or send a card. But, there are also those occasions when none of the above is possible.

Many years ago, I was giving a parish mission in the Midwest. Once in a while when I am giving a presentation, especially on a difficult subject like this one, and I am looking at the faces of hundreds of people, I begin to wonder if anything I am saying is sinking in and making a difference in their lives.

Maybe that is what Jesus meant when He said, "Blessed are those who believe but cannot see." (John 20:29)

After a session on forgiveness, I met two amazing women. I will call them Mary and Martha. I was standing in one corner of the church praying for people and offering spiritual direction. A woman with tears in her eyes literally fell into my arms and began to weep. She kept saying, "thank you, thank you." When I asked her why, she looked up at me and said, "Tonight I finally forgave the man who murdered my father 25 years ago."

Wow, I didn't have to wonder very long if the Holy Spirit was moving in lives that night. I asked her, "After so many years of suffering, why tonight?" She said, "I realized that for 25 years I have given that man the power to hurt me everyday. Tonight I forgave him and took the power back."

Not more than ten minutes later, another woman approached me and gently pulled me aside, because she didn't want anyone to hear what she was about to say. "Deacon, tonight I forgave the man who raped my daughter 15 years ago. I have a peace that I never thought I would ever have again."

By those women forgiving those men, will they ever forget what happened? NO! When they forgave, were they validating the actions of those men? NO! Did they communicate their forgiveness in person? NO! Will they ever establish or re-establish a relationship with those men? Probably not!

Did it take courage and grace to do what they did? Absolutely! They left that church experiencing the abundant life that Jesus Christ offers each one of us: His peace, hope, joy, love, faith and healing, the fruits of the Holy Spirit.

Can't Vs. Won't

Linda and I are certified spiritual directors. Over the years, we have met with hundreds of people in need of guidance in their spiritual lives. In fact, we strongly encourage all people who want a strong spiritual foundation to find a good, experienced spiritual director.

I would say that for the majority of the people who have come to see us, unforgiveness is at the core of why they are sitting in front of us. They may not know it when they first come in, but by the time we peel the onion layers of their lives, it becomes very evident.

I hear over and over, as people begin to open up and share their hearts: two words, "can't" or "won't'"

I used to fall into the "won't" category. I understood what forgiveness was and what my Lord Jesus Christ was telling me to do, I just wouldn't do it. At first, many years ago, I was somewhat puzzled when people would say they can't forgive, and later it became crystal clear to me what was going on.

Let me give you a personal example of what I mean. Two weeks after Linda and I were married, I was sitting in our living room while Linda prepared dinner. Amazing aromas were coming from the kitchen and I was ready for a five-star meal. Then I heard those words, "Honey, it's time for dinner." I jumped up and proceeded quickly to the table, ready to enjoy a sumptuous meal.

She put the dinner on the table and there was an eerie silence. I looked at it and said, "What is that?" Not a good thing to say as a newlywed. Linda said, "It's a casserole!"

I was 22 years old and I can honestly say that I had never seen a casserole. I grew up in a family that was strictly meat and potatoes and all the food had to be individually placed on the plate. What I was looking at was a dish with everything mixed together. I proceeded to say, "What am I supposed to do with this dinner?" I think Linda had a couple of ideas on what I could do with it.

She said, "Grab the spoon, scoop it up, put it on the plate and eat it!" When I followed her directions and ate the casserole it was amazing. Today casseroles are one of my favorite meals! You see, I could spell and say the word casserole but I had never seen one so I had no clue what it was or how to approach it.

It is the same with forgiveness. Most people can say and spell the word forgiveness, but over the years, I have encountered so many people who have no idea what it is or how to apply it to their lives. They grew up in a family, or a situation, where forgiveness was never practiced or modeled, and therefore they don't know what it is or how to approach it.

When we begin to explain in very basic terms what forgiveness is and the blessings it will produce for them, it is like an epiphany and a new beginning in their lives.

Two Brothers Set Free

Over the years, Linda and I have had the opportunity to see and experience so many amazing healings and resurrections in people's lives.

At a recent retreat, I asked everyone gathered in the church a final question before closing with a prayer.

"At this moment, is there anyone in your life, past or present, that God is asking you to forgive and be merciful to?"

Remember, the definition of mercy is giving someone what they don't deserve.

The following evening, a man came up to me before the start of the session and asked if I remembered the question I asked everyone last night.

"Of course, I remember," I said. He went on to say that as soon as the question was asked he knew who it was for him. He told me it was his brother that he hadn't spoken to in over 30 years.

I said, "Thirty years, what did your brother do to hurt you?" With tears welling up in his eyes, he quietly confessed, "I couldn't remember what he had done."

I gently took his face in my hands and I said, "What are you going to do?"

"At that point, a big smile came across his face and he told me with great joy, "Deacon, I have already done it!" He went on to share that when he got home after the retreat that night he immediately went through a box of old family papers and ran across a tattered phone book. It had his brother's phone number listed.

He called the number, not knowing if was still the right one. As soon as he heard the voice on the other end, he knew it was his brother and he began to cry uncontrollably. When his brother realized that after 30 years he was hearing the welcome voice of his estranged older brother, he also began to weep.

With great pain, this man said to me, "Deacon, one of my brother's children died and I didn't know it. His wife had cancer and I was not there to help him. I feel so heartbroken."

I told this gentleman that he can't change what happened in the past, but he and his brother can have a new beginning in their relationship.

Before the retreat was over, he told me he had purchased airline tickets to see his brother and family the following month.

As I watched him walk out of the church, knowing I would never see him again, I thanked our almighty, sovereign God for the mercy and compassion he had shown my brother in Christ.

In this chapter, we have tried in very basic and practical ways, to explain what the Biblical and spiritual principles of unforgiveness, forgiveness and reconciliation are, and how they apply to your life.

We have used scripture, our own personal faith stories and examples of people just like you and me.

You now have the opportunity to act on what you have read.

With great love, understanding and compassion, allow me to lead you on a prayerful examination of your conscience. You will have the opportunity to forgive anyone in your life, past or present, who has hurt or offended you.

Please find a place that you would consider comfortable and remove any distractions. Approach the following pages in a prayerful manner.

As I mention various people, it can be helpful to imagine and visualize them in the presence of our Lord.

Ask Him to give you the grace to forgive.

Begin With An Examination Of Your Conscience

Lord Jesus, I ask for the grace to forgive everyone in my life. I thanks you Lord that you love me more than I love myself, and that you want my happiness more than I desire it for myself.

Lord, I choose now to forgive myself, for my sins, faults and my failures. I forgive myself for anything I have done to hurt you or anyone else. Lord, I know that if I am truly sorry that you already have forgiven me. Today, I forgive myself.

Jesus, please forgive me for the times I have been angry, bitter or resentful towards you. When I blamed you Lord for the hard times, the financial difficulties, the sickness and even the death that came into my family, please forgive me.

Lord Jesus, I choose now to forgive my mother and father for all the times that they may have hurt me. I forgive them for any lack of support, love, affection or attention. And please forgive me Lord, for the times that I hurt or sinned against my mother or father.

Jesus, I forgive my spouse or ex-spouse for any lack of love, affection, consideration, support or attention. I forgive them for their faults, weaknesses, hurtful words and actions. And please forgive me, Lord, for any time or in any way I have ever hurt or sinned against my spouse or ex-spouse.

Lord Jesus, I choose now to forgive my brothers and sisters for the times they may have hurt me, resented me or competed for my parents' love and affection. I forgive them for the times that they may have physically or emotionally harmed me. And please forgive me Lord for all the times that I hurt or sinned against my brothers or sisters.

Lord Jesus, I forgive my children and grandchildren for any lack of respect, obedience, love, attention, warmth or understanding. Lord, please forgive me for all of the times I have hurt my children and grandchildren.

Lord, I forgive all my relatives who have interfered in our family and brought dissension and confusion. I forgive them for the times they hurt my spouse, children or me. And please forgive me, Lord, for the times I hurt or sinned against them.

Jesus, I forgive my co-workers, employer, former employer or employees for the times they gossiped about me, hurt me in any way, or would not cooperate. I forgive them for the times they were disagreeable or made my life miserable in any way. Please forgive me, Lord, for the times I was guilty of those same sins.

Lord, I forgive any professional people for the ways they may have hurt me. I forgive doctors, nurses, lawyers, police, firefighters, principals, teachers, social workers and politicians. And, once again, please forgive me for the times I hurt or sinned against any of them.

Lord Jesus, please forgive me for not seeing others as my brothers and sisters, and as temples of the Holy Spirit. Lord, please forgive me for my prejudice, bias, bigotry and using or abusing other people. And please forgive me for my sins against them.

Jesus, I choose now to forgive any bishops, priests, deacons, sisters, religious and any member of my church community for the ways they may have hurt or sinned against my family or me. I forgive them for their weaknesses, faults and failings. And please forgive me, Lord, for any ways that I have hurt or sinned against them.

Finally, Lord, I ask for the grace to forgive that one person who has hurt me the most, that one person I consider at this moment to be my greatest enemy, that one person I find hardest to forgive, that person I said I would never forgive. Lord, please free me of the burden of unforgiveness and fill my life with your peace.

Jesus, you know our needs. We want to be free of all our burdens. Drive out the darkness of unforgiveness and fill our hearts with your peace. Help me to forgive all of these people, including myself, and help me to accept your forgiveness. Amen.

At the beginning of this chapter, I said I would be leading you on a spiritual journey. I mentioned that at the end of this chapter there would be hopefully no misunderstandings about the teaching of Jesus Christ when it comes to forgiveness and reconciliation, and what He is calling us to do.

It now becomes a choice, a choice that you will act on now and quite possibly carry with you into eternity. Let's make it the right decision, one that pleases God and builds up His kingdom.

Linda and I are hopeful that the "spiritual power tools" that we have shared and outlined will assist you in building a strong spiritual foundation in Jesus Christ.

We hope you enjoy your journey!

Our Closing Prayer

Lord, we humbly come before you as your children and a community of faith. Please give us your love, mercy, healing and forgiveness in our time of need.

Grant us freedom and graces where we may be chained by resentment or unforgiveness.

Give us a new heart to love you so that our lives will reflect the image of your Son, Jesus Christ.

And may this world come to know, through our lives and churches, that He truly is the one you have sent, your Son, our Lord and Savior, Jesus Christ.

Amen.

Call To Action

1) Prior to your reading of this chapter, what was your understanding of forgiveness?

2) Currently, who are the person(s) in your life whom you are struggling to forgive?

3) What roadblocks are holding you back from forgiving them?

4) What specific actions might you take to remove those roadblocks?

5) As you read or prayed through the examination of conscience, did you forgive anyone? If so, who?

6) Is there anyone you are unwilling to forgive at this point? (Refer back to Question #3.)

7) Are you willing to do everything on your part to forgive?

Chapter 5

Bob Is Not The Real Hope

Back in the mid-1940s in America, one of the stars of the entertainment industry who helped the nation keep up its courage and hope during World War II was comedian Bob Hope. His efforts to keep the country's morale and hope high became an important part of surviving that global conflict.

But, today, the world's people face other serious threats and challenges. Even if Bob Hope was still around today, he never was the real hope for people. Even then, as today, the only real hope comes from our Savior, Jesus Christ.

But hope from Jesus comes to us through surrender.

Surrender and hope!

Yes, they really are connected. As followers of Jesus Christ, do we truly embrace the biblical reality of surrender?

We have all done things for which we are ashamed, and we live in the tension of who we have been and who we are yet to be.

Because our hope is in Christ, we can let go of bad choices and sins of the past, and look forward to what God will help us to become.

So, my brothers and sisters in Christ, don't dwell on the past, instead grow in your knowledge of God by concentrating on your relationship with Him now.

Realize that you are loved and forgiven and then move on to a life of faith and obedience. Look forward to a fuller and more meaningful life because of your hope in Christ.

Living a life of constant surrender and renewed hope is what our Lord wants for us each moment of our lives. Before we focus on the amazing theological virtue of hope, allow me to break open and outline some key points about surrender.

The dictionary defines surrender as "ceasing resistance to an enemy or opponent and submitting to their authority."

However, in the Christian mindset, surrender means giving and surrendering our life to the one who gave us life in the first place. Throughout our lives, our Lord asks us to surrender certain things. He doesn't do this for His benefit, He does it for ours. He knows that, if we will, we will truly find the hope and freedom that we desire.

Over my life I've had to make the decision to surrender many things to my Lord. For example, regret, guilt, shame, fear, anger, sin, bitterness, resentment and, believe me, the list goes on and on.

Now surrender is an ongoing process. It's not a one-time event.

Too often, when we take on this challenge, we immediately focus on the things we've already surrendered rather than focusing on the things we have yet to surrender. The Gospel of Jesus, the words of Jesus, teach us that when we give away our life, in other words, when we surrender our will, our wants, our needs, our desires to our Lord, it is than that we find life and hope.

Being an authentic Christian, and the key word here is authentic, is ultimately going to cost us our lives. That is why so many people are Christians in name only. When they begin to become aware of the cost and the price they are going to have to pay to follow Jesus, they just won't do it.

When we surrender, we are building up God's Kingdom. But when we refuse to surrender, we are building up our own kingdom.

For over 20 years, in my own personal life, I have used a process to let go and give anything to God, and it works!

I also use this process when I give spiritual direction.

I'd like to offer you this five-step process.

If you will use this in your life, you will be able to surrender anything that God has asked of you. It is my hope that you will use it to gain the abundant life and hope that our Lord wants for you.

The first step involves coming to an understanding that you have things, worthwhile things, to surrender. For you that might be a very simple step. You might already have come to the awareness that you have a lot of things to surrender, as we all do.

However, some people have a very hard time getting past this first step. They are people that I like to call perfectionists, people who like to be in control. I've learned that these folks will find this first step very difficult because people who are perfectionists, and like to be in control, always believe that they can fix anything.

So when they come to an understanding that there is something in their life they cannot fix, that they can't control anymore, and that they have to give it to God, it becomes a very difficult thing for them.

So the first step is to come to an acceptance and understanding that you have things to surrender.

Step two is simply to name it, name the things you have to surrender in your life. Just make a list. Don't try to analyze it, don't try to figure it out, just name it.

Now for step three.

Begin to imagine what your life would be like if you were not carrying those burdensome things around with you everyday. Think of the peace, joy, love, hope, and freedom that you would begin to experience.

Once you've done that, and once you begin to realize how great your life would be if you would just dump these things and give them to God, you should feel an eagerness to want to do this.

But then we come to the fourth step, which is asking yourself why aren't you doing it? Why aren't you letting it go?

Until you can come to that understanding, you will never be able to surrender.

For most people, this is the most difficult step.

Quite often, a good spiritual director is needed to help you peel the onion to uncover the reasons you're not letting go.

Once you've gotten to that core reason why you're not letting it go, and deal with it in a healthy way, then you come to the fifth step, which is to make a firm decision to let it go and give it to God.

I hope this five-step process will help you to surrender whatever it is that God wants you to surrender.

Let Us Focus Now On Hope

As we begin focusing on the main topic of this chapter, which is hope, let us focus our minds and hearts, calling upon our Lord to be with us in a very special way.

There's a story about St. Francis. One day as he was working in his garden, this man can running up to him. He said, "Francis, what if I told you that you only had three hours to live, what would you do?"

St. Francis pondered the question for a moment and then answered the man, "Well, I would just keep working in my garden."

You see, St. Francis had reached a point in his life where everything he did, no matter where he did it, was in line with the will of the Lord. So he was constantly at peace.

That is what each of us should be striving for, for each of us to become a saint, which simply means that our will and God's will are so united that they become one will.

Jesus said, "I have come to set the captives free."

What Linda and I have seen in our society over the last few years, and it just literally breaks our hearts, is an increase in hopelessness and a decrease in freedom.

Life without hope is empty. The gift of hope is as big as life itself. Hope is one of the three theological virtues, which are faith, hope and love.

When we lose hope we are no longer free. We become captives.

Jesus came to set us free.

What is so interesting with this virtue of hope is that so many Christians get off track because they confuse worldly hope with Christian hope.

The world's view of hope is often expressed as, "I don't know what's going to happen, but I hope something happens."

Let me say that again, because this is where we can easily get off track.

The world's view of hope is often expressed as, "I don't know what's going to happen, but I hope something happens."

Christian hope is a confidence that something will happen because God said it would.

Christian hope is when God has promised us that something is going to happen and we put our trust and our hope in that promise. Hope is not a feeling, hope is not an emotion. Christian hope is based on the knowledge that Jesus said it was going to happen.

And, as Christians, we are called to put our hope and all of our trust and faith in Jesus.

Now, our hope, trust and faith is not in where we're going. Our hope, our trust and our faith is in who we are following right now. If you are following Jesus Christ, right at this moment, then where you're going is exactly where you're supposed to be going.

The road may be bumpy. You may not be able to understand it. You may not be able to see the end of the road. But if you can honestly say that you are following Jesus Christ then you're going the right way.

But if you have to honestly say, "You know, I think I'm following someone or something else," then my brothers and sisters in Christ, stop what you're doing because you're not going in the right direction.

Let's briefly look at two scriptures that relate to hope.

Now when Jesus rose from the dead and ascended into Heaven, the early Christians believed that Jesus would return quickly. They thought He was going to come back right away.

The letter to the Romans was written by the apostle Paul 57 years after the birth of Christ. The letters to the Hebrews were also written by St. Paul just a few years later in 70 A.D. In this time span between 57 and 70 A.D., the Christians of that time were beginning to see that the return of Jesus was not going to happen as quickly as they thought. They were beginning to question, they were beginning to doubt.

Also, these Christians were undergoing fierce persecution, spiritually, physically, emotionally as well as financially. They needed to be reassured that Christianity was true and that Jesus was, indeed, the Messiah.

In other words, St. Paul knew that he needed to be the cheerleader of hope. He needed to give these early Christians something to hang on to, hope.

Please pick up your Bible and turn to the Letter to the Romans, Chapter 15, verse 13. Remember this is the Word of God, the living Word of God, so what these words mean is as important to you and me today as they were to the people that St. Paul spoke to over 2,000 years ago.

"May the God of hope," there's that word hope, "fill you with all joy and peace in believing, so that you may abound in hope by the power of the Holy Spirit."

If you are wavering at all in your belief in the words of Jesus Christ, right now as you read this book, then listen again to these words from St. Paul because they are meant for you.

"May the God of hope fill you with all joy and peace in believing, so that you may abound in hope by the power of the Holy Spirit."

My brothers and sisters in Christ, we are Easter people. We are called to be filled with hope. They world we live in is falling apart. Jesus said it would fall apart. We do not live in a world that's filled with hope. We must find our hope in Jesus.

Remember, Jesus is the anchor of hope in our life. The interesting thing about an anchor is that it is either going to save you or it is going to sink you. Right now, who or what is your anchor?

As Christians, our anchor must be Jesus.

Now, turn to the letter to the Hebrews, Chapter 6, verses 17 and 18. Again, the words of St. Paul are meant for each and every one of us today, just as much as they offered hope to the people of his day.

"When God wanted to give the heirs of His promise an even clearer demonstration of His purpose, He intervened with an oath (remember that word, oath) so that by two immutable things in which it was impossible for God to lie, we who have taken refuge might be encouraged to hold fast to the hope that lies before us."

St. Paul was telling the Christians then, and he's telling the world today, that's you and me, that God gave us an oath and that God does not lie.

Knowing that should give us hope.

Remember what I said Christian hope is. When God has promised that something is going to happen, you put your trust in that promise from God. It is a promise that will happen, because God said it would happen. As St. Paul said, God gave us His oath and God does not lie.

Those two scriptures, in the midst of whatever storm you might be going through, in the midst of a world that's just falling apart, our hope, trust and faith remains in God because He said it.

We must reach a point in our spiritual journey where we say to ourselves, God said it, I believe it and I'm going to act on it. It may not make any sense but, if you look at the lives of all of the saints over the centuries, you'll see that they each reached a point in their lives where they said, "Jesus said it, I believe it and I'm going to live it!"

That's one of the aspects of our faith that gives me hope.

I'd like you to take a moment and think of the plight of the eleven Apostles after Jesus was crucified and died. Remember, Judas had gone off and killed himself, so there were now only eleven Apostles remaining.

After Jesus was killed on that cross, they all ran in fear to the Upper Room, where they had shared in the Last Supper with Jesus. Filled with paralyzing fear, they locked the doors because people wanted to kill them.

Can you begin to imagine what these Apostles must have been going through? They had put all of their trust, hope, and faith, in fact they had put their entire lives, into following Jesus Christ.

It's easy to imagine these eleven men in this Upper Room saying to each other, "How do we get out of this with our lives? How do we escape? How do we get home to our families and our friends?"

But, that's not what happened.

Do you honestly believe that these eleven men, after experiencing all of the things that they had gone through with Jesus, would have then gone out to the ends of the Earth, been persecuted, beaten, thrown into prison, run out of town and ultimately killed for a dead man?

Absolutely not!

What happened?

Jesus appeared to these eleven men in that Upper Room. And when Jesus appeared, their fears vanished and they were filled with hope. They realized, at that moment, that Jesus was who He said He was, that everything He said and taught and preached was true, and they realized it was for them.

Then, they did what Jesus asked them to do. They went out and proclaimed the teachings of Jesus Christ, The Good News!

So, the question arises, why do we lose hope? It is a common, human thing that people, at times, lose hope. We lose hope because so often we focus on the closed doors in our lives, and we don't see the ones that God is opening for us. If we are focused totally on the closed doors in our lives we are going to lose hope.

Right now, Jesus has closed some doors in your life. He has closed them because they're supposed to stay closed. But, at the same time, He's opening new doors, opportunities for new beginnings.

Which doors in your life are you looking at? If you feel yourself losing hope, then you're focusing on those closed doors.

Now, let's look at another scripture that talks about whether we're looking at the closed doors or the open doors.

This is a scripture we've heard many times but I'm offering you some insights, insights that I had missed for a long time even with repeated readings. Perhaps you have, too.

Please turn to the Gospel of John, Chapter 11, and look at verses 1-6, verse 17, verses 20-27 and verses 39-44.

That scripture says "Now, a man was ill. It was Lazarus from Bethany, the village of Mary and her sister, Martha."

You may recall that Mary was the one who had anointed the Lord with perfumed oil and dried His feet with her hair. It was her brother Lazarus who was ill. So the sisters send word to Jesus, saying, "Master, the one you love is ill."

When Jesus heard this, He said, "This illness is not to end in death. It is for the glory of God that the Son of God may be glorified through it."

Now, Jesus loved Mary and her sister, Martha, and Lazarus. But, when He heard that he was seriously ill, He still remained for two days in the place where He was."

Let's move down to verse 17.

"When Jesus arrived, He found that Lazarus had already been in the tomb for four days."

Now, in verse 20, the Bible tells us that when Jesus was coming, Martha went to meet Him and said, "Lord, if you had been here my brother would not have died. But even now, I know, whatever you ask of God, God will give you."

Jesus said to her, "Your brother will rise."

Martha said to Him, "I know he will rise, in the resurrection on the last day."

Now this is one of the very few times while Jesus walked this Earth that Jesus told somebody who He was. Jesus told her, "I am the resurrection and the life. Whoever believes in me, even if he dies, will live. And, everyone who lives and believes in me will never die. Do you believe this?"

Martha said to Him, "Yes, Lord, I have come to believe that you are the Messiah, the Son of God, the one who is coming into the world."

In verses 39-44, Jesus said, "Take away the stone."

Martha, the dead man's sister, said to Him, "Lord, by now there will be stench. He has been dead for four days."

Jesus said to her, "Did I not tell you that if you believe you will see the Glory of God?"

So, they took away the stone and Jesus raised His eyes to Heaven and said, "Father, I thank you for hearing me. I know that you always hear me but because of the crowd here I have said this, that they may believe that You sent Me!"

And, when He had said this, He cried out in a loud voice, "Lazarus, come out!" The dead man came out, tied hand and foot with burial cloth and his face was wrapped in a cloth. Then, Jesus said to those around Him, "Untie him and let him go."

Now, let's look more closely at this gospel of our Lord. At the very beginning of this scripture, Jesus said, "This sickness will not end in death but it is for the glory of God."

You see, Jesus knew what He was going to do. Even when He found out that Lazarus had died, He still waited two days before going to him. Remember, we serve an "on time" God. Jesus was not a minute early, Jesus was not a minute late, Jesus was right on time.

When Jesus arrived at the tomb, He was surrounded by people who had lost hope.

Why? They were focusing on the closed tomb and not the open door that Jesus was offering. They did not see or understand the promise that was coming down that dusty road.

Now, when He got to the tomb, scripture says that Jesus wept. A lot of people think that Jesus was grieving because His friend Lazarus had died. I don't think that was why He was weeping. Jesus knew before He got there what He was going to do.

I believe that Jesus was weeping because He was surrounded by people who had lost hope. These people are calling Him Lord, but they had lost hope. He was weeping because He wanted to say, "How can you call me Lord and, at the same time, lose hope?"

And nothing has changed for 2,000 years.

I believe today that when we say, "Jesus, you are Lord," but at the same time we have no hope, Jesus weeps.

Martha, at that moment, had reached a crossroads of overwhelming circumstances. Her brother had died. And, despite her faith, these circumstances were clashing with the theology in her head, her belief system, and it was becoming very personal.

Are You Facing Challenges To Your Own Faith?

That may well be the same thing that's happening to you right now. There may be some overwhelming circumstances in your life that are just butting up with what you say you believe.

Are you facing doubt or some circumstances in your life where Jesus is taking everything you say you believe and driving home the same questions He asked Martha?

Today He is asking us, "Do YOU believe this? Do YOU believe that I truly am Lord and Savior and Messiah and that no matter what circumstances are happening in your life, I can overcome anything?"

So my question to you, as you read this book, is do you believe?

Twenty-nine years ago, I came face-to-face with this scripture in my own life.

A whole series of events hit my belief system head-on.

Linda and I began having problems in our marriage and our marriage began falling apart. I filed for divorce. But Linda stood on the promises of Jesus. These circumstances were butting up against what we said we believed. With our marriage falling apart, there was pain, there was hurt.

But Jesus was looking at both of us and saying, "Glenn, Linda, do you believe this?"

Maybe your marriage is falling apart. Maybe your kids are doing things you never thought they'd say or do. Maybe a dear friend of yours has just been diagnosed with a terminal illness. Maybe you have been diagnosed with a terminal illness.

Maybe you've lost your job or maybe you can't find a new job, maybe you're running out of money. And all of these horrific circumstances are clashing with what you believe.

However, where you're sitting right now, Jesus is looking at you and saying, "Do you believe that I'm who I say I am? Do you believe that my promises and teachings are true? Do you believe that they're for you?"

You see, this is where the rubber meets the road. It is very easy to praise the Lord, and it's very easy to call Him Savior and Messiah when everything is going great. But how powerful it is when we call Him "Lord" when things are going wrong.

Pope Francis recently said, "It seems that so often our churches are not only places of worship but they're also hospitals, where people are deeply hurting."

Over the last two decades that Linda and I have traveled all across the United States and Canada, giving retreats, and missions, and conferences, I've confirmed Pope Francis' statement. We see wonderful, beautiful people sitting in those pews, but many of them are hurting, deeply hurting.

Let me give you a true example of what I'm talking about. Many years ago we were giving a parish mission in a small Southern town. As is my custom, I preached at all of the Masses before that mission started.

At one of the Masses, I walked down the center aisle with the priest and went to my appropriate chair. I was sitting there as an opening song was being sung and I saw a woman, let me call her Mary, who was sitting in the front pew with her husband and her two children. She was weeping uncontrollably. That woman wept from the time the Mass started until the Mass ended, and never stopped crying.

She was in church, but she was a broken, wounded, hurting soul.

After the Mass I went up to the priest and asked him why that woman was crying.

"Well," he said, "about six months ago she was driving down a rural country road at night when a little boy ran across that road, and she hit him. Unfortunately, that little boy died."

Everyone told her it was an accident. It wasn't her fault. Even the child's parents had forgiven her and said, "Mary, it's not your fault."

But Mary would not forgive herself.

Mary had lost hope.

All she could do was cry.

Surprisingly, Mary came to the first night of that mission. But, once again, no matter what I said, she cried from the time it started until the time it ended. For three days she came to our mission, and each time Mary cried the entire evening.

On the last night, amazingly, Mary walked into that church, looking extremely sad, but she wasn't crying. At a certain point in the evening I sang a song, and I invited everybody to close their eyes and to focus on the words of the song. That song was "Amazing Grace."

As I started to sing the song, with my eyes closed as well, I heard a voice. I thought to myself, is that really someone's voice or is it just my imagination? I opened my eyes and to my amazement, I saw Mary standing in the front pew. She was not crying, not sad, but with a big smile on her face and her arms raised, she was singing along with me.

That moment was as close as I have ever witnessed Jesus raising somebody from the dead.

When Mary walked into the church the first night of that mission, she had no hope. She was spiritually and emotionally dead from grief, guilt, and hopelessness. But Jesus, with His amazing grace and unconditional mercy, healed Mary of her hopelessness.

And, He set her free.

You see, she was a captive in her mind because she had no hope. But Jesus set Mary free.

When the mission was over, Mary came up to me and put her hands on my cheeks.

"Deacon," she said, "I have my hope back!"

Remember, life without hope is empty. The gift of hope is as big as life itself. At that mission, Mary realized that Jesus is who He says He is.

So I'm asking you, wherever you are right now, to put your trust, faith and hope in Jesus.

If you're ever losing hope, or if you've lost hope, you can tap into the amazing, abundant grace of God, right now, twenty-four hours a day. It's there for you. Grab a hold of it, use it and allow Jesus to set you free.

Once again, I want to thank you from the bottom of my heart, for reading this fifth chapter, "Bob Is Not The Real Hope." By now we realize that Jesus, and only Jesus, is the real hope!

Our Closing Prayer

In the name of the Father and the Son and the Holy Spirit.

Lord, we thank you for being with us in moments like this. Lord, we thank you for giving us Your Word and for loving us the way that You do. Give us the grace to surrender those things that keep us from the abundant life.

Instill in us, Lord, the desire for hope, the gift of hope, that we may be willing to make the choice that hope is your will for our lives, that we will begin to act on it with every breath and every action that we do.

We thank you, Lord Jesus, for dying on the cross for us, for your unconditional mercy, in spite of who we are and what we do every day. Lord, please, lift us up with your power and protect us with your love.

As always, we ask these things in the name of our Almighty Father God and your Son, our Lord and our Savior, Jesus Christ.

Amen.

A Call To Action

1) After reading this chapter, do you embrace the Christian mindset of surrender?

2) At this point in your life, what are the things God is asking you to surrender?

3) Are there any closed doors in your life right now? What are they?

4) What areas of your life do you want or need renewed hope?

5) Are you willing to put your hope in the risen Christ? If so, how?

Chapter 6

Seize The Moment!

The overall content of this book has focused on how to use various biblical principles, what Linda and I call "spiritual power tools," to assist you in building a strong spiritual foundation in Christ, even long after you have finished reading this book.

As we have stated several times, when we as Christians want to know the truth about a spiritual or moral principle, it is important that we learn from the master teacher, Jesus Christ.

In your Bible, please turn to the Gospel of Matthew, Chapter 7:24-27. Jesus says, "Everyone who listens to these words of mine and acts on them will be like a wise person who built his house on rock. The rain fell, the floods came, the winds blew and buffeted the house but it did not collapse. It had been built solidly on rock.

"And everyone who listens to these words of mine but does not act on them, will be like a fool who built their house on sand. The rain fell, the floods came and the winds blew and buffeted the house and it collapsed. It was completely ruined."

Once again, Jesus does not mince words. As I look back over the first 35 years of my life, I was primarily the "fool" who built his house on everyone and everything other than Jesus and His Gospels.

Jesus preaches and teaches about two foundations. He is very specific about what will happen if we follow His instructions, and He is equally as clear about what will occur if we build our foundation on someone or something other than Him and His teachings. We all have a choice about who and where we will build our spiritual foundation. These are the two promises I mentioned in the first page of the Introduction to this book.

Let's break open the words of Jesus in greater detail and depth. There are three words that always jump out to me when I read and reflect on this scripture passage. The first word is "everyone." It is not meant only for a select few, but for all humanity.

The second word is "listens." I have discovered that there is a difference between hearing and listening. We hear with our ears, but we listen with our hearts. Jesus is asking us to take His words and place them in our hearts, so they can transform us into the person He created us to be since the beginning of time. St. Benedict calls it, "Listening with the ears of our hearts."

And the third word is "act." We are supposed to do something with what He preaches and teaches. We should apply His teachings in our own lives, as well as in our marriages, families, workplaces, schools, neighborhoods and wherever God leads us.

After he had taught His Apostles everything His Father had instructed Him, Jesus told them to "Go and make disciples." "Go" was, and is, an action word!

Jesus tells us that if we will follow His instructions, that no matter how tough or difficult our lives may be, we will be jostled around a bit but our house will not collapse. As a reminder, this is a promise from God!

Have you ever known somebody who was going through a terrible struggle? Maybe it was a troubled marriage, a job loss, the death of a loved one or a tragic illness, yet they seemed to be able to go through it with a peace that was beyond all understanding. It is because they took the words of Jesus seriously. Before the hurricanes of life hit, and they hit us all, they took the opportunity to build their spiritual house on a rock, the rock of Jesus Christ.

But, Jesus also tells us that if we don't build our spiritual house and life on Him, our house will crumble. Another promise from God!

Throughout the pages of this book, Linda and I have been lovingly asking you to look at all the areas of your life, those areas that might need a change to help realign your focus so that you build your foundation according to Christ's will. Change is never easy.

To act on the teachings and commandments of God takes courage and commitment. But, remember, out of love for you and me, Jesus Christ made the greatest commitment that anybody has or will ever make when He went to the cross and died for our sins, for our redemption.

I believe that if we could truly understand, in the depths of our hearts, what that commitment of Jesus really meant and still means today, there isn't anything that we wouldn't do for Jesus.

Simply going to church for an hour on Sunday would not be enough. We would go anywhere He asked us to go. We would give up and surrender anything He asked because of His love, forgiveness, mercy and commitment to us on that cross.

Throughout this book, Linda and I have offered you many ways to deepen and strengthen your spiritual foundation in Christ: surrender; finding God in all the situations of our lives; mercy; forgiveness; faith; unconditional love and hope.

But how do we take these spiritual and moral principles and weave then into the fabric of our everyday lives?

You don't have to be a scripture scholar or theologian to do so. However, you do have to have the desire and want to create the time to enrich your life in ways that keep you close to your Savior, Jesus Christ, even in a world that wants to chew you up and spit you out.

Let's seize the moment, open our tool boxes and explore five additional powerful and practical "spiritual power tools."

I want to emphasize that these important tools I'm offering are not simply my own ideas. I'm only expanding on what is written by a spiritual leader of our Catholic Church, Saint John Paul II, in a small book entitled, **"On the Coming of the Third Millenium."** He wrote it to help all people prepare and celebrate 2,000 years of Christianity. The Third Millenium has arrived and we are well into it at this point.

To me, these tools and steps appeared at first to be simple to understand, but very challenging to implement because of my already busy and hectic life. However, I had reached a crossroads in my life. I knew that if I wanted a deeper relationship with

Christ, a better understanding of my faith and a stronger spiritual foundation, I would have to carve out some time by rearranging my priorities. In other words, I had to change!

Now I would like to make you a promise. If you will begin doing these five "spiritual power tools" everyday, yes, everyday, I promise your life will be better and have deeper meaning. Why? Because they will lead you on a path that will take you closer to Jesus Christ and His abundant and amazing graces.

As I have stated in the early pages of this book, Linda and I would never ask you do to anything that we haven't done or aren't currently doing ourselves. I practice and use these five tools each day. As a married couple, Linda and I try to do them everyday. We are living witnesses that they will change your life, strengthen your marriage (if you are married), deepen your faith and bring your family closer together.

You can also use these tools if you are living a single life, whether widowed, divorced or not yet married. Jesus did not come for married couples only, He came for each of us individually. No matter our station in life, we each have minds, hearts and lives that Jesus can enrich, if you let Him, if you will invite Him in.

(1) PRAY EVERYDAY!

There are 24 hours in every day and 168 hours in every week. That never changes. Let me ask you a question, a question I have often asked myself. Out of a 24-hour day, how much time do you spend in prayer? An hour? Less than an hour? More than an hour?

Once again, Jesus sets the example for us when it comes to prayer.

The Bible records Jesus praying 25 different times during His earthly ministry. He was continually in a prayer mode. He prayed when He was alone (Matthew 14:23), in public (John 11:41-42), before important choices (Luke 6:12-13), before meals (Matthew 26:26), before and after healing (Mark 7:34-35 and

Luke 5:16) and to do His Father's will (Matthew 26:36-44), among other things. Jesus also taught on the importance of prayer (Mark 11:24-26, John 14:13-14 and Luke 6:27-28), including the Lord's Prayer (Luke 11:2-4 and Matthew 18:19-20).

If you read all of the above examples, you will have an excellent outline of why we should pray. If it was important for Jesus Christ, it should be important for those of us who call Him Lord.

A wonderful aspect of prayer is that our Lord is not so concerned with how we pray, meaning the specific form of prayer, as much as His deep desire that we communicate with Him. We can pray while driving, while walking or jogging, even while doing the dishes or washing our cars. There are countless opportunities to pray each day.

The Word of God also lists many types of prayer. Here are just a few examples: prayer of agreement, where two or more people stand in agreement regarding a certain prayer (Acts 2:42); prayer of intercession (1 Timothy 2:1); prayer of faith (James 5:15); prayer of thanksgiving (Psalm 95:2-3); prayer of worship (Acts 13:2-3) and prayer of petition or request (Philippians 4:6).

The Catholic Dictionary defines prayer as "The raising of the mind and heart to God." It has always helped me to think of prayer as plugging into the divine power source, God's power, which is available to all of us anywhere and anytime. We simply need to connect and plug in.

To emphasize my point, you know you can walk over to the switch on the wall of your home and easily turn the lights on or off. However, if you turn the switch to the "off" position and the lights go out, the main power source remains on ready to activate the lights again with a flick of the switch.

My brothers and sisters in Christ, there is evil in the world, simply turn on the television news, listen to the radio or read the newspaper. But there is also evil we cannot see or hear. Because of those realities, I would never leave my home without being grounded in prayer.

Many years ago, I became concerned that I never saw my children pray, until I realized they never saw me pray. They would see me sit for hours in front of the television or computer but my two daughters never saw me pray. As parents, we are supposed to be the primary examples and educators of our faith and all its aspects to our children. I wish I could have a "do over" with my children when it comes to the Biblical and spiritual aspects of prayer.

Let's kick it up a notch and begin to pray each day - serious, honest and consistent dialogue with God. Try that for 30 days and it WILL change your life!

(2) HAVE A RENEWED APPRECIATION OF THE WORD OF GOD

Once again, the Catholic Dictionary defines the Bible as "The collection of books acknowledged by the Christian community to be written by human authors under the divine inspiration of God. It is the uncompromising and indivisible source of revelation given by God for the salvation of humankind."

For the last 30 years, it has been my road map, my spiritual GPS system, keeping me on track and out of the ditch.

Growing up as a child, our family had one of those large Bibles with the gold-edged pages and the six-inch letters on the front cover which spelled out "Holy Bible." It sat on our coffee table in the living room. It was the cleanest thing in the house. My Mom would dust it everyday.

She had to dust it because no one in the house would dare pick it up. Periodically though, I would pick it up and my Mother would slap my hands and say, "Don't touch it!" I began to associate pain with the Bible. I used to say, "That book hurts." I stopped picking it up. It became like a museum piece.

As I grew older, I had people, mostly in my church, tell me not to read the Bible because I would never be able to understand it, the pastor would tell me what I needed to know. Therefore, I found the time each day to read countless magazines and newspapers, but never found the time or had the desire to read the Bible, which is God's inspired and written word sent to guide, encourage, nurture, support and help us in our daily lives.

If God did not want us to read, learn and implement it in our lives, why would He have created it?

Let me be very specific with you, "DO NOT LET ANYONE CONVINCE YOU THAT YOU ARE NOT SUPPOSED TO READ THE BIBLE!" Our Lord left us His Words thousands of years ago so we would know how to live our lives, and how to interact with Him.

As Linda and I travel North America giving our missions and retreats, we actually hear people say, "I don't read the Bible because I don't understand it, but I live it." Yikes! How can a person live something they don't understand or have never read?

We have it so much easier than those early Christians. They didn't have beautiful, leather-bound Bibles. They had to wait for one of the Apostles to show up and share Jesus Christ and His Word.

Nothing should get in the way of reading the Holy Scriptures. If we have time to watch television, use our computers, read a magazine or newspaper, we have time to read, learn and implement God's Word in our lives.

A recently published study found that by the time a person reaches the age of 18, they will have watched the equivalent of four years of television. Now where and how do you think their minds and values will be formed and shaped? If they do not have the blessing of growing up in a family that prays together and is influenced by God's Word, their lives and minds will be formed and greatly influenced by what they see and hear on television, computers, cellphones, video games, movies and from their friends.

But the family that prays and reads God's Word together and attends church services weekly will experience the positive, strengthening, spiritual influences of Jesus Christ as a counterbalance to the values of the world.

(3) HAVE A GREATER KNOWLEDGE OF THE CATHOLIC FAITH

Now, if you are not of the Catholic Christian tradition, you might be inclined to skip over this third "spiritual power tool." I would urge you to continue though, because it will help you on your spiritual journey. Whatever your faith tradition may be at this time in your life, I would hope you would want to gain a greater knowledge and understanding of what the Catholic Christian church teaches and professes.

I reached a point decades ago where it was no longer acceptable to me to say I was a Catholic simply and only because my Mother was Catholic, or her mom was Catholic. Although I have countless generations of Catholics in my family, I had to "own" my faith! I also got repeatedly frustrated when people would ask me why I believed this or that about the Catholic faith. Most of the time I would say, "I have no idea. Someone 30 years ago told me that I had to believe it, however, I don't really know why."

As Catholic people we are called to know what it means to be Catholic. There was a time in my life, growing up in San Diego, California, that I loved professional football and the San Diego Chargers was my team. I could have told you from memory every statistic about each player on the Chargers team. Do you know how much work, time and effort it took to learn that?

But, at the same time, I hoped that my children would not ask me to name the 10 Commandments or the seven Sacraments, or any other aspects of my Catholic Faith, because I wouldn't have known the answers.

However, on Sunday morning, I'd be in the front pew standing and proclaiming the Apostles or Nicene creed, which is our profession of faith, louder than anyone else in the church. But, after Mass had concluded, I would walk out of my church and disregard everything I had just stated and professed. After all, I had just given God one hour that week. What more did He expect from me?

I never prayed, never picked up and read my Bible or studied my Catholic Faith. How could I live something and then pass it on to my children and grandchildren when I didn't know anything about it? There goes that "do over" thing again!

At this point in my life, I want my spiritual roots to be grounded in prayer, the Gospel of Jesus Christ and the teachings of my Catholic Faith.

One of the best vehicles for knowing our faith is a small book called, **"The Compendium of the Catechism of the Catholic Church."** It is written in a question and answer format and contains 598 questions and answers about the Catholic faith. Each answer is no more than a paragraph. It is not written for scripture scholars or theologians but for regular folks like you and me. I try to read and digest one question and answer every day.

For the next 30 days, learn one new aspect each day about your Catholic faith, or whatever your faith tradition may be at this time.

(4) BE PROUD AND ENTHUSIASTIC TO BE A CHRISTIAN!

A number of years ago, I was invited to be a facilitator for an all-day retreat for 100 students at a Catholic high school. There I was, just me and 100 teenagers.

What made it even more challenging was that the retreat had been scheduled for the day before the Super Bowl. So, of course, many of those students came in with an "attitude." Most of them didn't want to be there, and honestly, neither did I.

Well, after about 30 minutes of trying to get them settled and focused into this retreat, I asked these teens how many of them could tell me the name of the quarterback of the Green Bay Packers? The Packers would be one of the teams in the Super Bowl the next day. To my amazement, all 100 students raised their hands. They wanted their friends to notice that they knew the answer and they each wanted me to call on them.

Then I asked another question that was more relevant to why we were there that day. I asked how many students could name the four Gospels in the Bible? Not one student raised their hand. I decided it was time for a break.

I went over to the water fountain and this young man proceeded to follow me. I later found out he was a senior and the quarterback for the school's football team. He leaned down and whispered in my ear, "Matthew, Mark, Luke and John." I looked at him and said, "Son, why didn't you raise your hand? Why didn't you answer the question?" He said, "Deacon Harmon, I didn't want anyone to know that I knew the answer."

I was stunned and heartbroken. Which is worse, not knowing the answer or knowing and being ashamed to say it for fear of being ridiculed or rejected?

The next day, I turned on the Super Bowl and saw 50,000 screaming Green Bay Packers fans wearing their Styrofoam cheese heads. They were proud and enthusiastic to be a Packers fan and they didn't care who saw them or how ridiculous some people might think they looked.

I found nothing wrong with their excitement for their football team. As an ardent football fan, I could certainly understand and appreciate their enthusiasm.

However, I began to wonder how many of those proud and enthusiastic football fans who were Christian would be willing to wear a small cross on their shirt or coat letting everyone know that they were proud and enthusiastic to be a Christian?

Or, how many of those who were Catholic Christians would be willing to wear a Crucifix on a neck chain or make the sign of the cross the next time they went to dinner in a crowded restaurant as they asked God's blessing on their meal, making an outward sign of an inward truth, that they were proud to be a Catholic.

Now, I don't believe I am being unfairly harsh or judgmental. Please realize that there was a time when I would never do that in a restaurant. I went to my Catholic church every Sunday, but I did everything I could to hide the fact that I was a Catholic

Christian man the rest of the week. Why? Because I didn't know my faith and I was concerned that if people knew I was Catholic, they would ask me some aspect about the Catholic church, and I knew I wouldn't know what to tell them. All of us tend to share and talk about topics we are knowledgeable about, as well as being proud and enthusiastic. Those topics always become part of who we are.

Later, as my faith began to mature, I discovered that the more I read and studied the Word of God and my Catholic Faith and became more knowledgeable about those topics, the more proud I was to be a Catholic Christian man. Never forget that Jesus Christ was not ashamed to bleed and die on the cross for you and for me.

In conclusion, I urge you to be proud and enthusiastic to be a Christian man or woman. Do it in such a way that if someone asked you if you are a Christian and you smilingly respond that you are, they will reply, "My goodness, you certainly are proud to be a Christian, aren't you?"

ABSOLUTELY!

(5) SERVE

The Catholic Dictionary defines service as, "The exercising of one's duty toward God and neighbor. The first three commandments encompass one's responsibility of serving the Lord through prayer and worship. The final seven commandments are concerned with one's vocation to serve others through charitable works and good example."

In the Gospel of Matthew, Chapter 20:28, Jesus says, "Such is the case with the Son of Man who has come, not to be served by others, but to serve, to give His own life as a ransom for others." Once again, Jesus has set the example for us.

Although I have come a long way in my understanding of service to God and my church, when I hear God asking me to serve and help in some way, I am still at times quick to reach into my grab bag of excuses and say, "Oh Lord, I am so busy, tired and my back hurts. Please ask somebody else."

I don't believe that God is impressed.

What kind of a church do we want to leave our children and grandchildren? We all have gifts and talents that are meant to be shared to help and build up the Body of Christ in our faith communities and neighborhoods.

As I studied the early Christian church, which was established by Jesus and spread by the Apostles, I discovered an amazing aspect of those early faith communities. It was understood and accepted that if you became part of a Christian community, you had to become actively involved in serving others and you were expected to put everything you owned, all of your money and possessions, in the pot, so to speak.

The Apostles, as leaders and elders of the early church, would distribute the money and goods as they determined. The amazing thing about that approach was that everyone's needs were met.

That approach would seem outrageous in today's societies and even in today's churches. Despite 2,000 years of salvation history so many people have embraced the philosophy of get it, take it, grab it and once you have it, never let it go.

In a recent study in the United States, the results indicated that in most churches in this country, regardless of the denomination or faith tradition, only two or three percent of the people who come to church regularly are involved with their time, talents or treasure. In other words, you have two or three percent trying to meet the needs of 100 percent of the people.

Christ and His Apostles never meant for the Christian church to operate in that manner and mindset.

Often, I have people say to me, "Glenn, I'm too old to serve others." I will admit that at times age can be an obstacle, but most likely it is an excuse. Do you realize that Moses was 80 years old and Abraham was 75 when God called them? They were sitting back collecting social security! But, when they said "yes" to God, in spite of their age, difficulties, infirmities and struggles, with God's help and guidance they did mighty works for God's Kingdom.

We all have gifts and talents given to us by almighty God. They are to be used for His glory and the betterment of His church and society. My brothers and sisters in Christ, we have a Savior and His name is Jesus Christ. He is greater than any evil, stronger and more powerful than any difficulties or hardships we will ever face in this world.

If you will use the five "spiritual power tools" we have outlined in this chapter, along with the other spiritual principles found in the pages of this book, you will be well on your way to understanding and living the promises of our Lord by building your spiritual foundation on rock, the rock of Jesus Christ.

As we come to the conclusion of this chapter and the book, Linda and I hope and pray that our words have inspired you to be more prayerful and live more closely to our Lord, Jesus Christ.

If you have approached these messages with an open mind and heart, willing to receive whatever God has for you, we believe that you have been made aware of areas of your life you should change or improve. Please take these lessons, insights and inspirations that you hopefully have received and begin living your life with a deeper commitment and love for Jesus and your faith.

Please go out and make a difference in your own life and the lives of your family, friends, neighbors, co-workers, church members and people you encounter wherever God leads you.

Go out and "seize the moment!" Whatever blessings come from your efforts, please give God all the glory and honor. He has been the one who has and will continue to supply all your needs.

Enjoy the journey!

Our Closing Prayer

Loving, gracious and merciful Father, we thank you for being with us every moment of every day.

Help us to become more aware of your abundant and amazing graces.

Lord, open our minds so we can understand you in new ways. Soften our hearts so that we can experience you in deeper and more profound ways.

May our Lord uplift you with His power and protect you with His love.

May He return to you 30, 60 and 100-fold the help and blessings that you need the most in your life.

May your spiritual foundation be anchored in the Gospel of Jesus Christ and may our almighty, loving and forgiving Lord bless you in the name of the Father, Son and Holy Spirit.

Amen.

A Call To Action

1) As you began to read this book, where was your foundation grounded and anchored? Be specific and honest.

2) If your foundation is not currently anchored in Jesus Christ, what can you begin to do that will accomplish that goal?

3) Which of the five "spiritual power tools" are you currently using each day?

4) Knowing the commitment Jesus Christ made to you by dying on the cross, how might it challenge you to make a stronger commitment to Him?

5) Is there anyone you are meant to share this book with? Pray about it.

CPSIA information can be obtained
at www.ICGtesting.com
Printed in the USA
FSOW02n0818080216
16572FS